Travel Wise with Children

101 Educational Travel Tips for Families

Mary
Rodgers
Bundren

inprint
Publishing, Inc.

3

Travel Wise with Children
101 Educational Travel Tips for Families
Mary Rodgers Bundren
Inprint Publishing, Inc.

Design and Production:
Walker Creative, Inc., Oklahoma City, Okla.
Travel Wise with Children, Inprint Publishing, Inc.
and art elements in this book are registered trademarks of Inprint Publishing, Inc.

ISBN number 0-9645685-3-5
Library of Congress Catalog Card Number 98-71473

To order *Travel Wise with Children,* contact:
Inprint Publishing, Inc.
306 S. Bryant, Suite C-152
Edmond, OK 73034
(405) 340-1404
e-mail: explore@oklahoma.net

ACKNOWLEDGMENTS

Many thanks to the following people who provided help, encouragement, vision, and humor to make this book possible: Sarah Taylor, author, publisher, and friend, who was the first to believe that we could launch this project; Kristie Kay Bunney, M.A., early childhood development specialist, whose natural connection with children has, through example, inspired me to be a better mother and write a better book; Suzann Ham, businesswoman and early childhood educator who knows her business, and her business is childhood; Theodore A. Rees Cheney and Hazel Rowena Mills, my editors; Randy Yates, graphic designer; the creative staff at the Wallis Group, including Suzanne Fitzgerald Wallis, Ashley Allen, and Melani Hamilton; Lynn Price, my friend and writing colleague who opened many doors for me; and my many friends who opened diaries and memories of travel anecdotes, especially Debbie Carpenter, who has accompanied me on some of my most memorable journeys. I also want to thank my children's dedicated teachers at Holland Hall School in Tulsa, Okla., who have given me an education along with my children.

Most special thanks to my supportive family and to my parents, Lee and Mary Joyce Rodgers, who took four children and a dog across the desert in a station wagon without air conditioning, along with many like adventures, and were the last parents in the neighborhood to buy a television. We become what we learn in childhood.

This book is dedicated with love to my favorite traveling companions: Clark, Johnathan, Michelle, and Kara.

In Praise of *Travel Wise with Children*

"This is a wonderful book packed with useful tips and inspiration. This book will help parents build strong families and encourage them to have more fun with their kids."

Dr. Mary Pipher, author of *Reviving Ophelia*

"Before you make your hotel reservations, reserve this book at the library or bookstore. It can turn you family trip into a learning experience and seriously curtail the level of child 'whining.'"

Jim Trelease, author of *The Read-Aloud Handbook*

"Hands-on experiences serve as one of the most powerful motivating techniques for children to learn. This is a wonderful book that will provide an invaluable resource to parents as they discover a variety of ways to turn field trips, vacations, and other outdoor trips into exciting learning ventures. The ideas are realistic and can be easily applied by parents. I am certain that this book will be read and reread by parents as they seek information to turn family outings into fun-filled, exciting learning experiences."

Dr. Robert Brooks, Harvard Medical School Psychologist and author of *The Self-Esteem Teacher*

"In *Travel Wise with Children*, parents will find many creative ideas that not only make great family memories but also enhance their children's learning."

Cheri Fuller, nationally-noted speaker and author of *Unlocking Your Child's Learning Potential* and *Teaching Your Child to Write*

"Travel equals learning equals fun is the attitude of this new book—which applies to all kinds of family travel, from day trips to extended adventures."

Teresa Plowright, *travelwithkids.miningco.com*

In the beginning of this record I tried to explore the nature of journeys, how they are things in themselves, each one an individual and no two alike. I speculated with a kind of wonder on the strength of the individuality of journeys and stopped on the postulate that people don't take trips—trips take people.

John Steinbeck, *Travels with Charley*

Contents

Part One

• •

Travel Wise Preparation   19

Part Two

● ●

Travel Wise on the Road, In the Air, Once You're There   66

Part Three

· ·

Travel Wise Making Memories   141

Part Four

. . . .

Travel Wise Anytime   154

Part Five

. . . .

Travel Wise Resources   170

Observations From an Early Childhood Educator

During my first twelve years of school, I figure that my teachers offered a total of less than six uninterrupted hours in the marvelous natural laboratory at our doorstep: the Indiana dunes, a hodgepodge of buried forests, quaking bogs, and mountains of sand. Even in a place so well-suited for nature study, my teachers kept us inside classrooms for a thousand hours for every one hour they took us into the field.

Gary Paul Nabhan, *The Geography of Childhood: Why Children Need Wild Places,* Gary Paul Nabhan and Stephen Trimble

● ●

I remember the day I got my commercial driver's license. That sounds an odd assignment for a teacher, but one of my jobs has included driving a small bus of excited preschoolers on weekly field trips. I believe in introducing my young students to the many wonders of the community so they can "see" and "do" firsthand. Together, we've visited museums, submarines, factories, libraries, parks, Christmas-tree farms, construction sites, and just about any place where children can learn in safety. I've taken my two daughters on family vacations coast to coast because my "field trip" philosophy extends naturally to family outings, as this book points out. These field trips, no matter how simple, spark children's imagination, enhance cognitive development, and promote enthusiasm for life and learning.

This book is exciting because it blends two of my long-held beliefs about children: that they learn *best* by experience, and that the parents' role is irreplaceable in shaping these experiences. As an educator and parent, I've used many of the suggestions in this book on a daily basis to prepare my students and daughters for all kinds of excursions, and to enrich the experience as we travel—and after we return.

I support the book's emphasis on family connections during traveling. As an early childhood development specialist, I've worked with many families from all backgrounds, often emphasizing the importance of the parents' role in teaching values, supporting cognitive development, and being role models for social interactions and emotional health. It's a role unlike any other. But having worked with many families, I've grown concerned about the lack of family time in children's lives. This book offers many ways for parents and children to really talk, play, learn, and experience places together away from daily distractions.

The book also communicates the importance of early learning in a relaxed manner. Children don't benefit from pressure to learn, perform, or grow up too quickly. We are reminded that fun and education can and should be interchangeable. From simple neighborhood walks to full-blown vacations, each excursion can have a significant impact on a child's growth and development.

I especially like this book's simple format, which helps the reader remember that the travel process is far more than just the few days you're traveling. Children will delight in preparing for the trip and capturing memories upon returning. These creative tips set the stage for memorable learning experiences for the whole family.

Kristie Kay Bunney, M.A.
Early Childhood Development Specialist

From the Author

My friend Suzann told me a story which illustrates many truths about traveling with children. When her now grown (and very successful) children were school age, she took them to the King Tut Exhibit, then in Seattle. She was very excited to see the splendid display, having visited Egypt previously. Unfortunately, her children didn't share her enthusiasm. The farther she went into the exhibit, the grumpier her children became. The magnificent displays were overshadowed by "This is soooo boring!" and "How much loooonger do we have to stay here?" Sound familiar?

"I was just furious by the time we walked out," she said. "My viewing had been ruined, and I knew they hadn't gotten anything out of it."

Wrong, she learned later.

"Do you know that the following year, almost every report and school project they did had something to do with that King Tut Exhibit."

Many parents have had similar experiences, so it's important to keep in mind some basic travel truths as you wander through quiet museum corridors or along rocky mountain trails.

Travel Truth #1—The whole world is your child's classroom.

Travel Truth #2—Traveling is one of the best ways to enhance your child's education.

Travel Truth #3—Children absorb far more information than we as parents realize (even when they're complaining).

Travel Truth # 4—No child is too young to travel. You

just need to be aware of age-appropriate destinations and expectations.

Travel Truth #5—Traveling need not be exotic, expensive, far-flung, or elaborate to engage young, inquisitive minds.

Open up a world map and jump in with your children. This book challenges you to take your travel experiences one step farther by offering 101 Educational Travel Tips (while perhaps sparking some ideas of your own) to enhance both the vacation fun and your children's learning experience. Since I began traveling with my three children from the time they were born, I've been amazed at their knowledge of history, geography, and culture which blends with their academic studies. My friend Cindy's teenage son has an impressive knowledge of geography, and is always in the finals of the school geography bee. She credits the family's worldwide travels with his geographic interest. That's not to say that you have to travel to all corners of Earth to enhance your child's education, but you can turn your family vacation into the world's largest outdoor classroom experience.

Children are such natural, eager learners. You don't have to hit every museum in town to consider it a "learning" vacation. In fact, all vacations are "learning" vacations. Just observe a preschooler collecting shells along the beach or pouring sand on her toes, and you will observe an engaged young mind.

Your travel experience need not be elaborate. When my son was a toddler, one of his favorite "travel" experiences was walking around the block twice a week, watching and listening to the "gongy" (garbage) truck smash the garbage. We set our weekly calendar around the garbage-collection schedule. Along the way, he collected rocks, leaves, and even a few pieces of trash the garbage collectors had missed, a rather "academic" exercise for a toddler.

This book was inspired by travel experiences with my three children, but also by delightful travel stories from acquaintances, friends, and family. My three-year-old niece, Rachel, spent five weeks in England while her mother was teaching at a university near Manchester. A child already driven by the fantasies of Sleeping Beauty, castles, and princesses' dresses, she spent one night in a "real" castle in Wales that brought to life her make-believe castle world. What an experience for a three-year-old to be a princess for a night!

You certainly don't have to sleep in a castle to expose your child to the wonders of the world, but every girl should get to be a princess for a night, or an airplane pilot, astronaut, zookeeper, or whatever her imagination conjures. By traveling with your children, you can open wide those imaginations, offering glimpses of other cultures, topographies, histories, and climates. As you read the many educational travel games and opportunities, I think you will be amazed at how many you're already doing, and how easily you can incorporate them into your travel plans. It's not too difficult to buy a compass and let your child experiment in the backseat of the car. While he's experimenting, he's learning about direction, gravity, and magnetism, forces which control airplanes, ships, and much of the world around him.

In researching this book, I have consulted early childhood development specialists, schoolteachers, other traveling families, books, magazines, and the Internet. I watched for games, activities, crafts, and other opportunities that would challenge children to explore the world. My goal is to offer visual, auditory, and kinesthetic learning experiences that naturally incorporate language arts, math, science, history, and geography without a textbook, lesson plan, or desk. Whether you're visiting Grandma's, skiing down a mountain slope, riding the trolley through San Francisco, or simply strolling on a nature trail, remember that your children's minds are full of wonder. Stand back and watch as our vast earth, with its billions of years of history, freshly unfolds before them. Today's King Tut Exhibit can transform into tomorrow's research papers or careers, or at the very least, a great memory with a small corner of the world illuminated, and perhaps better understood. Happy exploring!

Mary Rodgers Bundren
May 1998

About the Author

Mary Rodgers Bundren has a master of arts degree in English from the University of Tulsa, and as a professional writer, her work has been published in many newspapers and magazines. She and her husband and three children have enjoyed many learning adventures while traveling. They live in Tulsa, Oklahoma. This is her first book.

How To Use This Book

• •

Travel Wise with Children is divided into five sections for easy use.

Part One: Travel Wise Preparation offers educational tips to prepare your children for their trip.

Part Two: Travel Wise on the Road, In the Air, Once You're There explores learning opportunities while you're on vacation.

Part Three: Travel Wise Making Memories highlights activities your children can do to preserve their trip experiences.

Part Four: Travel Wise Anytime brings the travel experience to your own backyard by offering tips to do at home.

Part Five: Travel Wise Resources offers books and activities to supplement the travel process.

Learning skills such as language arts, math, science, history, geography, temporal, mapping, organizational, and creativity are noted alongside the tip. The tips within each part are grouped by learning skill. Also noted alongside each tip is the appropriate age for the activity: preschool, early school age, school age, older school age, or all ages. This book is written for parents of children ages 3 through 14.

Symbols:

✏ Denotes tips adaptable to school and home-school curriculum.

📖 Denotes books and resources that I recommend highly.

Part One

● ●

Travel Wise Preparation

Ready! Set! You're almost ready to go! But before you leave, get prepared. Try these challenging activities to acquaint your children with their destinations. Most children are so excited about a family vacation, and anticipation is half the fun. This section provides learning activities to capture children's natural inquisitiveness by involving them in the trip-planning process.

✎ Travel Tip 1

Destination Discovery

Planning Your Trip

- school age
- math, language arts, organizational, and geography skills

It's time to plan the family vacation, but there are as many opinions on the subject as people in the household. Although no household needs to be a democracy, involving your children in vacation planning can be great fun and mentally challenging. Pose to the children the question, "So where do you want to go for vacation?" After you eliminate the "out of the question" destinations, invite your children to "sell" you on their travel plans. Tell them you're playing the role of consumer and they'll need to persuade you on their travel plans. You may need to explain up front that you reserve the right to make the final decisions, but you want to see their "sales presentations." Help them check out books about their destination, scour the Internet, visit travel agencies, write for information from tourism departments, and check travel magazines. Encourage them to make visual displays and budgeting charts (see Tip #17 for more budgeting details). When the research is complete, call a family meeting for Presentation Day. Discuss the details, but most importantly, praise your children for a job well done. How you make the final destination decision is up to you, but even if their site is not selected, they have learned some valuable skills and everyone has gotten some great geography lessons.

Getting from where you are to somewhere else is an adventure. This is true of physical movement but also of emotional, spiritual, or other travel. Going 'to' implies dynamics, more possibility. To me, the word destination sounds a thud of finality. I'd rather be on my way 'to' and have potential, than 'at,' where discussions are in the past tense.

Stephen Binns, "Road Reflections," from
Alaska Passages, edited by Susan Fox Rogers

✎ Travel Tip 2

Cutout Picture Books

- **preschool, early school age**
- **creativity and language arts skills**

supplies: paper (white or colorful construction), scissors, glue, markers, stapler with adult supervision (or some kind of binder), pictures of planned trip

Most preschoolers love creative art projects. Visit your local travel agency to collect brochures of your destination. Clip pictures of your destination and places you might visit along the way from travel magazines and brochures, or ask your destination's visitors' bureau to send information.

Encourage your young children to make a picture book introducing the rest of the family to your destination as well as sights along the way. With help, they can label the pictures. Your children will be delighted when they eventually see for themselves a building/beach/mountain/museum/animal/

waterfall that they have included in their picture book. In fact, the book can be used as an "I spy" game. They can put a star at the top of every picture they locate along the way.

✐ Travel Tip 3

Traveling by the Book

- **all ages**
- **language arts skills**

Wonderful stories, literature, fables, and biographies abound within the literary traditions of each state and region of the country and world. Visit your library and bookstores to discover books by authors from and subjects about the region/state you will be visiting. When we were planning a family vacation to Alaska, I bought a copy of Jack London's *Call of the Wild* to read to my children before the trip. There are many children's stories, fiction and nonfiction, which will illumine the travel experience. Please refer to Tip #101 for a list of excellent books related to the region/state of your destination.

✎ Travel Tip 4

A Word to the Wise

Travel Vocabulary

- **all ages**
- **language arts skills**

Traveling is a great way to increase your child's vocabulary. Whether you're a spelunker dodging the stalactites and stalagmites deep in a cavern or a deckhand on a catamaran flying across a windy lake, your trip will expose your child to many new words, phrases, local idioms, and dialects. What's "pop" in one part of the country is a "soda" elsewhere. Some regions might argue that Cola is neither, it's a "soft drink." My friend told me that when she and her family moved to a new state, her daughter's new friends called her "Soda Pop" because she came from "pop" country and had moved to "soda" country.

Make a list of new words and phrases your child might encounter on the trip. Include historical names, locations, animals, people, and everyday words which might be unfamiliar. Have your child keep a list in her journal of new words and phrases that she learns. Billboards, newspapers, and local magazines are good ways to find new words and phrases. On the trip home, play games with her new vocabulary. What are some synonyms? Rhyming words? What is the funniest word? Take the longest word and see how many other words can be made from the word.

Variation: Every time she sees a word from her list on a billboard or printed anywhere, she collects a bingo chip (which can be any small item you've brought along: paper clips, candy pieces, pennies). Perhaps she can exchange her bingo chips for a special souvenir toward the end of the trip.

✎ Travel Tip 5

Bear Hunt

Story Improvisation

- preschool
- language arts and creativity skills

We're going on a bear hunt,
We're going to catch a big one,
What a beautiful day!
We're not scared.

So begins the classic children's story *We're Going on a Bear Hunt* by Michael Rosen. The children in the story encounter all manner of difficult circumstances: tall grass, a river, mud, a forest, until they come face to face with a bear, and scamper quickly home. Check out the book at the library and use the story for improvisation and travel role playing. Change the bear-hunt destination to Grandma's house, a big city, the beach, or wherever your travel plans may take you. What will you see along the way? How will you get there? What might you encounter? Encourage your child to collect props for their improvisational trip. Other books which will encourage improvisational travel play include *The Runaway Bunny,* Margaret Wise Brown; *Oh, The Places You'll Go,* Dr. Seuss; *Arthur's Family Vacation,* Marc Brown; and *Emma's Vacation,* David McPhail.

Travel Tip 6

Pack 'n' Play

Packing Your Bags

- **all ages**
- **creativity, organizational, and math skills**

Involve your child in the packing process. The younger the better. Let her gather some of her own clothes. Even preschoolers can count out several pairs of socks and shorts. Encourage pretend play. Give her an old suitcase to pack clothes for a doll or stuffed animal for an imaginary trek to their favorite destination, say, Grandma's house. Let her pack her own backpack with personal choices of books, tapes, and snacks. Preschoolers will love the responsibility of collecting a few belongings such as toothbrush, comb, and a favorite stuffed animal, doll, or blanket. Take her to the store to purchase a few items for her backpack. Older children might receive some discretionary money for new purchases to add to their backpacks. They'll learn more if they price shop and follow a budget.

Variation: Your young child might want to designate a travel "friend" such as a stuffed animal to accompany her on her journeys, along with a log to record the many travel adventures of her "friend." Take a picture of her with her travel companion on each journey to put beside the written record. She might also want to loan her "friend" to vacationing classmates to increase her "friend's" travel experiences.

On a recent trip to Maui, my daughter brought Shiny, a traveling stuffed bear originating from an elementary school in Fort Worth, Texas. The bear had made its way to my daughter's school and she was thrilled to take Shiny with us on our trip. Shiny visited the Haleakala Volcano at sunrise and was a great deckmate on the *Trilogy* catamaran for a snorkle excursion to Molokini, a volcanic island near Maui. We took a picture of Kara and Shiny sitting in the captain's chair aboard the catamaran for Shiny's classmates in Texas to enjoy. Coincidentally, one of Kara's classmates was also vacationing on Maui, and we arranged to exchange Shiny with Mont so he could take Shiny for the remainder of his vacation. Through the trip, Shiny became quite a special travel companion for the whole family.

• •

For my part, I travel not to go anywhere, but to go. I travel for travel's sake. The great affair is to move.

Robert Louis Stevenson

✎ Travel Tip 7

By George!

Famous Acquaintances

- school age
- language arts, geography, history, and organizational skills

History's movers and shakers can be found in all regions of the country. Who were they and what have they contributed? Provide resources for your children to learn about famous people who herald from your destination. Play twenty questions with the family and see whether they can guess what famous paths you may cross. For younger children, obvious choices such as George Washington and Abraham Lincoln will be appropriate. Older children can research more obscure historical figures. A visit to the beach at Nags Head, N.C., might unearth the Wright brothers, who soared into fame a few miles down the road. Neil Armstrong stepped off the moon and into Ohio, along with fellow astronaut John Glenn. Olympic gold medalist Shannon Miller balances her life around Edmond, Okla., just a handspring away from fellow Olympic gymnasts Bart Conner and Nadia Comaneci, Norman, Okla., residents. Ask your children to tell the family about the famous people they've selected. Almanacs and encyclopedias will be good sources for your research.

Variation: Encourage your child to assume the persona of the famous person, and have family members interview them.

Variation for older kids: Have them collect ten or more famous names connected to your travel plans. In the car, play the twenty-questions guessing game. The game can be played for points, candy pieces, or just for fun.

* *

Book Resource Tip:

Many excellent biographies have been written for children. Check your local library or book store. Several biography and history series are listed in Tip #101.

Travel Tip 8

Sensory Experiences

Trip Audiotapes and Videotapes

- **all ages**
- **language arts and auditory skills**

Check out book audiotapes from your library or visit a new or used bookstore to select a few story tapes that your whole family will enjoy along the way. Make your own audiotapes of the stories listed in the resource guide (Tip #101) relevant to your destination. Nothing quiets car travelers faster than a good yarn that keeps the children absorbed.

There are many good videos of regional interest which can be checked out at the library or rented at a video store. Museums or gift shops at your destination will often sell videos difficult to find outside the region. They may be worth purchasing on occasion for your video library and to share with your child's classroom during a related unit of study. Once finished with the video, donate it to a school or city library.

Variation: Ask a grandparent or special friend to record a short book for children to listen to in the car.

• •

Resource Tip:

A friend told me how much her family enjoyed the audiotapes of the many adventures in Lilian Jackson Braun's cat mystery series.

Travel Tip 9
Music and All That Jazz

- all ages
- music, geography, and language arts skills

In *The Music Man*, Professor Harold Hill urged audiences to "Give Iowa a try." Rodgers and Hammerstein introduced "OOOOklahoma where the wind comes sweeping down the plains," and we all "Left our Hearts in San Francisco." Regional music appeals to all ages. Expose your children to music of the area you will be visiting. Of course, some regions are easier than others. It's hard to avoid the jazz influence in New Orleans, so let them dance to the beat of the fine musicians in Jackson Square. Visit Aspen, Colo., in the summer for the world-famous Aspen Music Festival. Visit recording studios at hands-on museums and stroll along outdoor cafés that musicians frequent. Music is all around you, and chances are that the music of your destination may be somewhat different from your music back home. Learn about mountain music, Native American, Hawaiian, and other multicultural music. The possibilities are as many as the miles.

Check out some regional songbooks from your local library and teach your children some of the songs. Encourage them to make a musical instrument to go along with the songs.

* *

Book Resource Tip:
American Folk Songs for Children, Ruth Crawford Seeger

(Doubleday), features 90 American classic songs along with suggestions for improvisation, rhythmic play, and games.

Jazz: My Music My People, Morgan Monceaux (Knopf)

Kids Make Music, Avery Hart, Paul Mantell (Williamson)

By the Dawn's Early Light: The Story of the Star-Spangled Banner, Steven Kroll (Scholastic)

Voices of History, Westward Expansion (CTP), includes two tapes with its historical songs and narrative.

Recommended tapes:

Wee Sing Around the Campfire

Wee Sing America

Wee Sing Fun 'n' Folk

States and Capitals, Rap, Rock 'n' Learn

States and Capitals, Twin Sisters Productions

Patriotic Songs of the USA, Melody House

Red Grammer's Favorite Sing Along

Rockin' Down the Road, Greg and Steve

A House for Me, Fred Penner

We're on our Way, Hap Palmer

Car, Trucks, and Trains, Kimbo

Folk Dance Fun, Kimbo

✎ Travel Tip 10

The Joy of Cooking

- all ages
- science, math, and language arts skills

A favorite reading-specialist friend cooks with her students. As she shops with them, she teaches them to read labels. As she cooks with them, she teaches her students reading skills from the recipe's many simple, repetitive words such as *cup, butter, sugar.* Several math teachers I know cook with their students to teach them fractions. Ask any child. Most would rather learn fractions in the kitchen than on paper in the classroom. So what does all of this have to do with traveling? Plenty! Use your upcoming trip to add a little regional flavor to your meals. Most libraries have an excellent selection of good cookbooks. Browse through and find some regional recipes to introduce your family to a different slice and spice of Americana. Your children can help prepare "An evening in little Italy," a "N'awlins jambalaya feast," or some of that three-alarm Texas chili. Go one step farther and add some appropriate background music and ask your child to make some festive place mats. The meal need not be elaborate. Cook up some fish sticks and rice, slice up a pineapple and coconut, use a beach towel as a tablecloth, check out some Hawaiian tapes at the library, and you have an instant luau. Exploring the culinary delights of a region might even expand the taste buds of your pickiest eater.

One of my daughter's favorite stories highlights regional cuisine. We were visiting friends in San Antonio when she was five months old. She was sitting in her walker on our friend's driveway and, as her father's back was turned, a preschool neighbor offered her a jalapeño pepper. As any five-month-old would do, she promptly put it in her mouth. The shriek was heard throughout the neighborhood. A baby who had not yet had her first rice cereal, she was a bit unprepared for a fire-hot pepper! She loves to tell people that her first solid food was a jalapeño pepper and watch their reaction. While you don't have to serve your kids hot peppers to sample the regional cuisine, you can point out the local products and food customs. If you're from flyover country, Maine lobster is a real delicacy. Pass the pralines, please.

● ●

Book Resource Tips:

♥ *How To Make an Apple Pie and See the World,* Marjorie Priceman (Dragonfly), a delightful preschool-early school age picture book to go with your cooking experience.

The Little House Cookbook, Barbara Walker (HarperCollins), has authentic recipes inspired by Laura Ingalls Wilder's *Little House* series.

✎ Travel Tip 11

"Ten, Nine, Eight...Blastoff!"

A Trip Countdown Calendar

- preschool, early school age
- language arts, organizational, temporal, and sequencing skills

supplies: large sheet of paper, crayons or markers, stickers or trip illustrations (optional), ruler

Anticipation is half the fun of your trip. Help your child make a Trip Countdown Calendar for the two weeks prior to departure. Since young children have little temporal concept of "two weeks" or even "two days," the calendar will provide a daily visual cue, showing the time left before departure. Each day, write down activities your child can do to prepare. Include packing and other small chores she can perform to help get ready.

Trip preparation ideas to fill your calendar might include a visit to the library to check out books, helping round up the animals for a trip to the kennel, sorting and gathering eight pairs of socks, packing her backpack, taking some perishable foods from your refrigerator to the neighbors, or filling the birdbath and bird feeder before you leave. Your child will enjoy decorating the calendar with stickers or trip illustrations. Each day, point out the day of the week, the date, and have her count how many days are left until departure. I remember saying, "Yes, that means you have to go to sleep five more nights before we wake you up really early to catch the plane."

* *

Fun Travel Facts

Wacky Laws in the United States
It's against the law:
- to slurp your soup in a public eating place in New Jersey.
- to holler *snake* within the city limits of Flowery Branch, Ga.
- to remove your shoes if your feet smell while you're in a theater in Winnetka, Ill.
- to buy ice cream after 6 p.m. in Newark, N.J., unless you have a written note from a doctor.
- to ride a bike into a swimming pool in Baldwin Park, Calif.
- for kids to buy lollipops in Spokane, Wash.
- for boys to throw snowballs at trees in Mount Pulaski, Ill.
- to push dirt under a rug in Pittsburgh, Pa.

Source: *Kids' Almanac,* Alice Siegel
and Margo McLoone Basta

Resource Tip:

Let your children think up some wacky rules for your town, family, trip, or destination.

"We can chew gum only when the sun is shining."

"Thursday is backward day. We must jump off the diving board backward, wear our ball cap backward, walk in the park backward."

"We have to sing 'Old MacDonald Had a Farm' every time we see a McDonald's."

✐ Travel Tip 12

Vacation Bulletin Board

- **all ages**
- **creative, organizational, and language arts skills**

supplies: bulletin board, tacks, construction paper, travel brochures, postcards or trip memorabilia, snapshots, and stickers

Use your travel plans as your theme and plaster your bulletin board with trip visuals collected from brochures and magazines before you leave, and as a "memento presentation" when you return. Take a picture of your child in front of his bulletin board to add to his trip scrapbook.

Resource Tip:

If your child does not have his own bulletin board, it is

easy and inexpensive to make in any size he chooses. Visit your local building-supply store and buy a piece of polystyrene foam board or Celotex board, any size, cover the board with any kind of fabric that matches the room decor, and hang it on the wall. You have an instant and attractive bulletin board. Of course, corkboard squares, premade bulletin boards, or poster board also work well.

Travel Tip 13

Relatively Speaking

Family Trees

- **school age**
- **language arts, geography, and history skills**

If you're planning a trip to visit family, it's a perfect time to acquaint your children with their extended relatives. No child is too young to begin learning about his roots. Pull out old photos and design a family tree. Or purchase a simple prepackaged variety for your child to fill in. Attach old and more recent photos so the family will be familiar with the relatives when you arrive. Another idea: Buy a map of the United States and put pictures of relatives in their respective states. Post the map so your child will have visual context of extended family.

How far back can you trace your family? What part of the country/world did your family originate from? How did you end up living in your town or city? What were their hobbies, careers? Take time to tell some stories about your ancestors' lives in a covered wagon, landing on Ellis Island, fishing in Louisiana bayou, panning for gold during the California gold rush. The oral tradition of storytelling used to be the method of communication between generations. Revive this wonderful art form and share your wealthy heritage with your children. Ask your relatives to become pen pals with your children. Before you leave, ask them to send pictures of their house, neighborhood, and pets to further introduce your children to their family.

● ●

Resource Tips:
Family History Activity Kit comes with family history activities, book, record book, family-tree poster, stickers, and cards (DK Publishing, Inc.).

Do People Grow on Trees? Genealogy for Kids and Other Beginners, Ira Wolfman (Workman)

Two great picture books about extended family include *The Family Reunion*, Tricia Tusa (Farrar, Straus and Giroux), and *The Relative's Game*, Cynthia Rylant (Aladdin).

✏ Travel Tip 14

Mapping Skills

- **school age**
- **geography, language arts, and math skills**

supplies: a map of the United States and/or your destination state, paper, pencil, ruler, stickers of flags, mountains, cars (see *Free Stuff for Kids*, Tip #101)

Although learning mapping skills may seem rather dry and academic, here are several suggestions to spark some cartographic interest.

Show your child a map of the United States and point out the key, explaining what the words mean. Ask him to draw a map of his room using some of the key words. He can make an overhead map, as a bird might view his room, or a view from his bed with direction and distance noted. Graph paper will help organize his scale. Next ask him to draw a map of his route to school. Which direction does he go? How many turns? If he could fly to school, how would he go? If he took a bike, how would that change his route? Show him the route you're planning to take on your trip. What direction will you be traveling? If you flew, how would you get there? If you drove, what is the best route? How long might each form of transportation take?

• •

Resource Tips:

A great Web site for all ages is MapQuest!, which shows the most direct route from your city to your destination.

Clip the weather map from the back page of *USA Today* or obtain some other simple U.S. map, laminate it and, with a washable marker, chart your route. You can decorate the map with state flag stickers, mountain stickers, etc. Encourage your child to take along the small map with her belongings and refer to it frequently as you pass through states and landmarks.

Rand McNally Sticker Atlas of the World has an "understanding maps" page and will provide hours of geography fun with reusable stickers.

Finding the Way: A Book and Craft Kit About Maps,

Mapmaking and Not Getting Lost, Creative Art Activities, Inc., (Creative Press).

• •

(Geography) is a subject too important to ignore because, as any mapmaker would tell you, "Without geography you're nowhere."
David Jouris, *All Over the Map*

✎ Travel Tip 15

Westward Ho!

Historic Trails

- **school age**
- **promotes geography, mapping, and history skills**

If you're planning a trip west, enter into the pioneer spirit and explore the historic trails along the way. Before you leave, check your library for some books about the great westward expansions in the eighteenth and nineteenth centuries. Some of the leading trails included:

The Santa Fe Trail, which stretched 1,000 miles from Missouri to Santa Fe and became the traders' thoroughfare for Yankee commerce.

The Oregon-California Trail, a beaten-down road leading pioneer families in covered wagons from Missouri to Oregon City or San Francisco during the 1840s and '50s.

The Pony Express, which started in Missouri and continued west to San Francisco.

The Klondike Gold Rush Trail, a route forged by gold fever that stretched from Seattle to America's last great frontier, Alaska.

The Mormon Trail, which took followers of Joseph Smith 1,400 miles across the prairies to Salt Lake City.

The Chisholm Trail, the cattle route from Texas north to Kansas along which ranchers and cowboys moved their cattle and settled "cow towns."

Take in some museums and visit landmarks along the pioneer routes. Of special interest is the National Historic Oregon Trail Interpretive Center near Baker City, Ore., where visitors can explore interactive exhibits and learn about the 350,000 emigrants who weathered the 2,000-mile journey. You can experience life aboard a prairie schooner on an Oregon Trail wagon train tour in Bayard, Nebraska, located along the original trail route. Contact Oregon Trail Wagon Train, Route 2, P.O. Box 502, Bayard, Neb. 69334.

* *

Resource Tip:

Oregon Trail computer games, MECC, ages 8 and up

The Oregon Trail, Leonard Everett Fisher (Holiday House), tells the story of the pioneers as they traveled 2,000 miles over the Oregon Trail.

* *

I do not remember crossing the Missouri River, or anything about the long day's journey through Nebraska. Probably by that time I had crossed so many rivers that I was dull to them. The only thing very noticeable about Nebraska was that it was still, all day long, Nebraska.

Willa Cather, *My Antonia*

Travel Tip 16
History Time Line

- school age
- sequencing, temporal, math, history, and language arts skills

supplies: roll of butcher paper, crayons or markers, illustrations (optional).

Every region of the country is rich in history. Take your child on a trip back through time, reliving the historical events that happened around your destination. Roll paper across a floor or attach it to the wall. Begin when the region was discovered, the town was chartered, or some other historical date, and move forward. Attach memorabilia or illustrations from the region, or encourage your child to illustrate his own interpretation of the historical events. Start with the earliest events and move forward. Bring the time line up to the present day to help him understand how long ago events such as the Revolutionary War, Civil War, Custer's last stand, or the California gold rush occurred. You can compare the history of your destination with your own region's history along the same time line. How much longer has your state been in the union than the ones you will be visiting on your westward trek? Plot the information on the time line. Roll up the time line and when you return, add more historical dates, along with memorabilia acquired on the trip.

✎ Travel Tip 17

Plan an Itinerary Game

- **older school age**
- **math skills**

supplies: a road atlas or map which includes your home, destination, and mileage between; highlighter, paper, pencil, and calculator (optional).

While parents ultimately plan and budget family vacations, children can be involved in several ways during the planning process. Encourage them to plan a sample itinerary. Supply your child with the following information: destination, budget, length of stay.

Sample game:
The Smith family is planning to take a five-day car trip to San Antonio from Oklahoma City. They have budgeted $950 for their vacation. Mrs. Smith asks her two children to plot the most direct route by car. They can see on the map that there are several possible routes. They calculate the quickest route based on mileage between cities and types of roads indicated in the key. Highlight the chosen route. Calculate the travel time to San Antonio. Mr. Smith needs to know how much gasoline will cost. The children calculate gas consumption based on number of miles to be traveled, miles per gallon, and gas prices. Mr. and Mrs. Smith ask the children to list needs and wants (perhaps the distinction between the two can be discussed) during their vacation to begin budget planning.

Their list includes:
- four nights' lodging
- three meals a day for five days (two days on the road) plus snacks
- tickets to Fiesta Texas Theme Park
- tickets to Sea World
- tickets to a water park
- spending money for miscellaneous shopping at Rivercenter Shopping Mall
- tickets for a river gondola ride
- visit to the Alamo

Once these needs and wants are recorded, the budgeting process begins. Mrs. Smith, who has several brochures from San Antonio, tells the children ticket prices on their wish list. Do they want to stay at a more expensive hotel with a bigger swimming pool and perhaps forfeit tickets to the water park? How much spending money is reasonable? Is the Alamo free? How much will food cost? Can they find a hotel with a continental breakfast included in the cost? Mr. and Mrs. Smith ask their children many questions to include them in the planning process. After the children discuss and calculate, they come up with the following budget:

- gas—$100
- lodging—$280, including 4 nights at $70 per night
- food—$390
- tickets and spending money for Fiesta and Sea World—$200
- Alamo—$0 (Perhaps they would like to make a donation with some of their trip money)
- spending money for each child—$25

Whether Mr. and Mrs. Smith follow the children's itinerary is up to them. But certainly, some of the children's wishes can be taken into consideration. This game is also fun to play with an imaginary itinerary. Begin by asking: "If I gave you $1,000 to take a trip, where would you go? How would you get there, and what would you do when you got there?"

When children have an emotional or time investment in a trip through planning and shared decision making, expectations and behavior may be more appropriate. And who knows? Future vacation plans just might spring from your young travel agents.

✏ Travel Tip 18

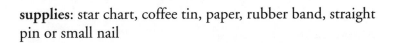

A Star Is Born

Stargazing with Your Child

- **all ages**
- **science and math skills**

supplies: star chart, coffee tin, paper, rubber band, straight pin or small nail

An outdoor trip such as a camping or beach trip is the perfect opportunity to teach your kids about astronomy and stargazing. Purchase a star chart at a nature or map store. Review what part of the sky you will be seeing on your trip and what constellations will be in view. Build your own planetarium with a coffee tin:

1. Remove the top and bottom of the can.

2. Secure a piece of paper with a rubber band over one end of the tin can.
3. With a pencil, draw the constellations by following the star chart on the paper secured by the rubber band.
4. Prick the stars with a pin.
5. Shine a flashlight up from the bottom of the can.

Presto! You now have your own planetarium to guide you in your star search. A young child can do this using only black construction paper.

Spend an evening stargazing on a clear night during your trip, preferably away from artificial lights. Can your kids recognize the constellations and name them? Are the constellations in the same position as at your home? How are they different? What makes their positions change? Can they find the North Star? Do all other stars seem to be rotating around it, as the earth rotates on its axis? Take along a small telescope for an even better view. You never know when a young Galileo might surface, armed with a coffee tin and stargazing map.

• •

Resource Tip:
Plan a trip to a planetarium during your travels. There are many fine ones throughout the country. *FamilyFun Magazine* recommends the Dorrence Planetarium, Phoenix, Ariz., Dr. Phillips CineDome in Orlando, Fla., Roger B. Chaffee Planetarium in Grand Rapids, Mich., Buhl Planetarium in Pittsburgh, Pa., and the Burke Baker Planetarium in Houston.

A Kid's Guide to Space Museums:

Neil Armstrong Air and Space Museum
1500 Bellefontaine Rd.
Wapakoneta, Ohio 45895
Astronaut Memorial Space Science Center
Brevard Community College
1519 Clearlake Rd.
Cocoa, Fla. 32922
Cernan Earth and Space Center
Triton College
2000 Fifth Ave.
River Grove, Ill. 60171
Henry Crown Space Center
Chicago Museum of Science and Industry
57th St. and Lake Shore Drive
Chicago, Ill. 60637
Kansas Cosmosphere and Discovery Center
1100 N. Plum St.
Hutchinson, Kan. 67501
National Air and Space Museum
Smithsonian Institution
Independence Ave. between 4th and 7th Sts., SW
Washington, D.C. 20560

Source: *Kids' Almanac,*
Alice Siegel, Margo McLoone Basta

Lightly Stepped a Yellow Star

Lightly stepped a yellow star
To its lofty place,
Loosed the Moon her silver hat
From her lustral face.
All of evening softly lit
As an astral hall—
"Father," I observed to Heaven,
"You are punctual!"

Emily Dickinson

✎ Travel Tip 19

Weathering the Weather

- **school age**
- **science and math skills**

supplies: weather map, outdoor thermometer, car thermometer

Weather is a great reason to travel. Whether you're a snowbird migrating south or a skier looking for snowy slopes, the weather can be a major factor in the success of your trip. Take travel time to encourage your kids to be weather watchers beyond the usual *sunny, cloudy, rainy* notations.

Activities:
a) Introduce your child to television's Weather Channel.

b) Buy copies of *USA Today* for several days prior to departure and show him the large, easy-to read weather map. Explain the weather symbols. Chart the weather of your destination on your Trip Countdown Calendar (Tip #11).

c) Install an outdoor thermometer at your home and in your car. Have your child read the thermometer for a few days prior to departure and keep a log of the temperature changes on your trip. As you drive to different elevations, ask your child to estimate the temperature differentials. Why does it get colder as you drive up a mountain pass or warmer at sea level? Ask your flight attendant what the outside temperature is as you reach cruising altitude. Why is it so much colder?

d) There's no business like show business, especially for kids. Give your kids some adult dress-up clothes, a weather map, a pretend microphone, and let them be your trip weather people. Ask them to report on the kind of weather they might predict for your camping, beach, or hiking trips. Pull out your video camera and videotape their weather segment. After all, many well-known entertainers began their careers as weather announcers.

• •

Book Resource Tip:
◆ *Weather Forecasting,* Gail Gibbons (Aladdin)
◆ *Thunder Cake,* Patricia Polacco (Paper Star)

Fun Travel Facts

Hottest and Coldest Temperatures on Record (Degrees F)
Hottest

134	Greenland Ranch, Calif.	July 10, 1913
127	Parker, Ariz.	July 7, 1905
122	Overton, Nev.	June 23, 1954
121	Alton, Kan.	July 24, 1936
121	Steele, N.D.	July 6, 1936

Coldest

-80	Prospect Creek Camp, Alaska	Jan. 23, 1971
-70	Rogers Pass, Mont.	Jan. 20 1954
-69	Peter's Sink, Utah	Feb. 1, 1985
-63	Moran, Wyo.	Feb. 9, 1933
-61	Maybell, Colo.	Feb. 1, 1985

Source: National Climatic Data Center

✏ Travel Tip 20

Up, Up, and Away

Exploring Flight

- **all ages**
- **science, language arts, and creativity skills**

Your child may be both excited and apprehensive about flying in an airplane. Particularly if this is her first flight, offer her a child-friendly glimpse of the mighty world of flight and what she might expect. Even if your child has flown right out of the nest, she will enjoy creative ways to learn more about that great big flying machine.

Activities:
a) There are many preschool and school-age picture books on the subject of airplanes and flight. Some of the many excellent choices include:
Airplane: And Other Airport Machines, Christopher Maynard (DK Publishing)
Flight: The Journey of Charles Lindbergh, Robert Burleigh (Philomel)
Amazing Flying Machines, Robin Kerrod (Knopf)
  School-age children will be fascinated with the intricacies of aircraft found in *The Ultimate Book of Cross Section,* DK Publishing, and *Incredible Cross Sections,* Stephen Bietsy (Knopf).
  ◗ *How To Fly For Kids,* Natalie Windsor (Corkscrew), is an excellent airplane companion book for young children.

b) Before your trip, organize a pretend corner filled with airline props such as pilot caps (these can be purchased in a learning store or catalog), an old blazer for a pilot or attendant's uniform, airline tickets (left over from one of your previous flights, or you might suggest that your child make his own with a hole punch and paper), blocks to build his own airport, airline wing pins collected from previous flights, plastic airplanes of any size, and a small suitcase to pack.

c) Encourage your child to make paper airplanes. Purchase a paper-airplane kit or give her a few sheets of old computer paper. Make several sizes. How does size change the flying patterns? Launch the airplanes on a windy day or in front of a fan. What happens? This is a great experiment to teach your older child about lift, thrust, drag, and gravity—the principles of flight.

d) Your child may enjoy taking a "friend" along to share her trip. Suggest she take a favorite stuffed animal that has never flown so she can educate her special friend with her new found flying knowledge.

● ●

I made an airplane out of stone....
I always did like staying home.

Shel Silverstein, *Falling Up*

✏ Travel Tip 21

Making Tracks

Train Travel

- **all ages**
- **science, language arts, and creativity skills**

Before my nephew Sam could talk, he was fascinated with trains. And he is not alone. From the pioneer trains of the Wild West to modern-day Amtrak, trains have held the imaginations of generations of children. I still remember my first train ride, in kindergarten, when we rode all of twenty miles and disembarked in the next town. It was the high point of the year. Take advantage of your child's natural curiosity about trains to explore locomotion. Check out some of the many great train books from the library and plan a real or imaginary train ride.

Activities:
a) Refrigerator Boxcar
supplies: refrigerator box, paint, knife to cut cardboard, props as desired

Obtain a refrigerator box or other large box from an appliance or department store. Help your child make a train car. Use your imagination. You can cut one of the rectangle sides off to expose the inside of the box to create the interior of a passenger or dining car. Paint wheels and train logos on the exterior of the box with craft paint. Set up props in the train car as desired.

b) Pretend Corner Props

Include the train in a pretend corner which might also include a conductor's hat, a train set such as Brio, Lego, or other commercial set, blocks to make "train tracks," and train tickets.

c) Trips

Plan a train trip as a part of your vacation. Amtrak has many scenic routes that cater to families. Some personal favorites include: the Durango and Silverton Narrow-Gauge Railroad, the Pikes Peak Cog Railway, the Georgetown Loop Railway, all in Colorado; the Cumbres-Toltec Scenic Railroad from Antonito, Colo., to Chama, N.M. Or try one of the many Amtrak train trips available throughout the United States

● ●

Resource Tip:

Trainorders.com is a comprehensive railroad Web site.

Trains

The railroad track is miles away,
And the day is loud with voices speaking,
But there isn't a train goes by all day
But I hear its whistle shrieking.
All night there isn't a train goes by
Though the night is still for sleep and dreaming,
But I see its cinders red on the sky
And hear its engine steaming.
My heart is warm with the friends I make,
And better friends I'll not be knowing,
Yet there isn't a train I wouldn't take,
No matter where it's going.

Edna St. Vincent Millay

• •

The Laugh Track

What is the best place to have a bubble-gum contest?
A chew-chew train
What did the engineer say when he saw the new locomotives?
'Diesel be fine.'
What runs all the way from New York to San Francisco without
moving?
Railroad tracks
How do you search for a missing train?
Follow the tracks.

Joanne E. Bernstein and Paul Cohen,
Riddles to Take on Vacation

✎ Travel Tip 22

Peaks and Valleys

Mountaintop Learning

- **all ages**
- **science and geography skills**

supplies: salt clay (recipe below), sturdy sheet of cardboard about two feet by two feet, tempera paint or food coloring, other decorations (optional)

My main memory of fourth grade (other than that my teacher was a southpaw like me) was the topographic map of the Swiss Alps that I made with salt clay. It was truly my most accomplished elementary-school project, and I still remember details of the Swiss Alps that I learned while sculpting my relief map. On a sturdy piece of cardboard, about two feet by two feet, I formed the mountains and the lowlands, based on pictures found in magazines. After the salt clay had dried, I painted the mountains, valleys, and lakes. Or you can add food coloring to the clay before molding it. Add even more details such as miniature cars, dogs, people, skis, trees, or any small props, handmade or purchased at a hobby shop.

If you're planning a mountain trek, spend some time before you start teaching your child about these unique geologic formations. After all, mountains cover one-fifth of the earth's surface. What mountains might you visit on your trip? How are mountains formed? What is the tallest mountain in the world? What is the tallest in North America? Name some North American mountain ranges and locate them on a map. Show your child a relief globe and encourage him to run his fingers over the mountain ranges. Explain that a relief map or globe shows elevations (peaks) and depressions (valleys). Can he tell by feeling the "bumps" which mountain ranges are the tallest? On your trip to the mountains, visit a local bookstore and learn about the particular mountains in the region. What's the history of the slope you're skiing on? How was it formed? Many ski instructors or trail guides can give you information on the geologic formations in the area. How is the mountain different in each season? What animals and plants thrive seasonally in the mountain habitat? Why do the trees quit growing at a certain elevation? Point out a tree line and the sparse vegetation above it. See Tip #19 to discuss mountain weather and temperatures.

Salt Clay Recipe:

2 c. flour   2 c. water

2 c. salt   2 T. oil

2 tsp. cream of tartar

Blend all ingredients together and cook over low heat until dough begins to stick together and form a ball. Dough should not be too sticky or crumbly. Cook about 3-4 minutes. Remove from pan and let cool. Knead. Store in an airtight container.

. . . .

Book Resource Tip:

◖ *The Sun, the Wind and the Rain,* Lisa Westberg Peters (Henry Holt), is a delightful picture book which illustrates the geologic concept of mountain building in a way children can understand.

Travel Tip 23

Oceans Away

Seaside Exploration

- **all ages**
- **science and geography skills**

When I was six, I decided I would grow up to be an oceanographer—a curious career choice since I lived in a landlocked state and had set foot in an ocean only once. It had nothing to do with wanting to study oceans and everything to do with the alluring pictures of marine animals and sea life published in *National Geographic.* I spent hours admiring sea creatures sashaying through the pristine depths, wishing I were swimming with them. If you're planning a trip to the beach, explore with your child the unique habitats of the world's oceans and their edges.

Activities:
a) In the bathtub or sink, play some floating and sinking games to introduce the concept of buoyancy.

b) Make a balloon-powered boat.
supplies: a bendable straw, a half-gallon milk carton, strong tape, scissors, a balloon, a nail

1. Cut one side off the milk carton.
2. Place the opening of the balloon over the end of the straw and secure tightly with tape.
3. Poke a hole in the bottom of the milk carton big enough for the balloon straw to go through.
4. Bend the straw at an angle.

5. Once inserted into the milk carton, blow up the balloon through the straw, and hold the end of the straw to keep air from escaping.

6. You're ready to launch the boat by letting go of the straw in the water. Make sure the straw end stays under water. Why does the air propel the boat in the water? Why does the milk carton boat stay afloat?

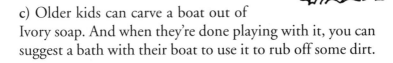

c) Older kids can carve a boat out of Ivory soap. And when they're done playing with it, you can suggest a bath with their boat to use it to rub off some dirt.

• •

Resource Tips:

The Beachcomber's Book, Bernice Kohn (Viking), offers craft ideas and seashore activities.

Where the Waves Break: Life at the Edge of the Sea, Anita Malnig (Carolrhoda), is a picture book that shows what treasures might wash up at the edge of the sea.

◼ If you're visiting the Hawaiian Islands, don't miss the new Maui Ocean Center, a splendid display of the tropical ocean habitat and its species. From velvety sea cucumbers to a Whale Discovery Center, the Ocean Center offers a hands-on tour of one of the richest environments on earth. The Maui Ocean Center's address is 192 Ma'alaea Road, Ma'alaea, Maui, Hawaii 96793. Its Website is www.coralworld.com/moc.

Fun Travel Facts

1997 Best Beach Ranking
1. Hulopoe, Hawaii
2. Kailua, Hawaii
3. Caladesi Island State Park, Fla.
4. Hamoa, Hawaii
5. Wailea, Hawaii
6. Cape Florida State Recreation Area, Fla.
7. Hanalei Beach, Hawaii
8. Kaunaoa, Hawaii
9. Fort De Soto Park, Fla.
10. St. Joseph Peninsula State Park, Fla.

Ranked by Dr. Stephen Leatherman,
Professor and Director, Laboratory for Coastal Research

✏ Travel Tip 24

Products R Us

- **school age**
- **geography skills**

What products come from the part of the country you will be visiting? Organize a household-product scavenger hunt. Your oatmeal may come from Chicago, your corn chips from Dallas, and your peanut butter from Boise. Where are all of these places, and will you be passing through? Check a map and note where the products originate.

United Designs in Noble, Okla., is the largest animal-figurine manufacturing company in the country and gives plant tours on weekdays. And there are hundreds more tour opportunities around the country. How do you find them? Partly through your household scavenger hunt. If your peanut-butter jar originates in Boise, chances are there's a big plant there. Also consult your library. Most travel guides offer information on area products and great tours.

In Oklahoma and Texas, football reigns, especially if Oklahoma is playing Texas. Every year, the governors of both states place a wager on the game's outcome. The wager is usually a state-made product which the loser sends in short order to his winning counterpart. It's good fun and advertises homegrown products. Your children can do likewise. If you're visiting friends and relatives along the way, your child can select a hospitality gift of a locally manufactured product or craft. Exchange yours for something from their region. How about some three-alarm Texas chili for some Vermont maple syrup? Tour some of your local manufacturing plants and purchase some appropriate gifts.

When my friends moved from New Jersey to the Chicago area, they wanted to acquaint their children with the local culture of their new home. They took in as many sights as possible, including a very sweet tour of the Jelly Belly Factory in North Chicago, a newsy tour of the *Chicago Tribune,* and a nuts-and-bolts tour of a GM assembly plant in Wisconsin.

• •

Book Resource Tip:

🔖 *Watch it Made in the U.S.A.,* Bruce Brumberg and Karen Axelrod (John Muir Publications). "Touring factories anywhere in the country is a fun experience for children. It can also be highly educational. Children will remember the smell of crayons, the taste of breads right off the production line, the sight of car- and paper-making machinery. And because they are kids, they'll be curious about how it all works," so explain the book's authors. This book is a true find for adventurous families. From Coke to Corvettes, Hershey's to Harleys, the book offers tour information on 300 factories across the United States.

Travel Tip 25

Travel Props

- **all ages**
- **math, science, and geography skills**

Compass

Before you leave, introduce your child to the compass rose on a map. Take a compass on a walk around the neighborhood or park and see how directions change. Trace a U.S. map on paper and give your child puzzles to solve. What is the northernmost capital other than Juneau? What is the southernmost point of the country? Which direction do the Rocky Mountains run? Find an east-west river. Sense of direction is a developmental skill that will come with maturation, but early exposure through fun games enhances many academic skills.

Stopwatch

Many stopwatch games can be invented (including timing your kids in the fifty-yard dash at a rest stop to discharge some pent-up energy). Use the stopwatch to time a mile on a four-lane highway, then on a two-lane highway or country road loping along behind a combine. How fast can you run a mile? How fast might a jaguar run a mile? When you stop at a restaurant and there's a fifteen-minute wait, have your child time the wait while you stroll along a sidewalk. Use the stopwatch to calculate how long it takes to drive a mile at 60 miles per hour. How about 70? How much faster will you make the 500-mile trip if you are able to average 65 mph rather than 55 mph? As an added benefit, this information might halt some unnecessary bathroom stops.

Calculator

Encourage your child to use a calculator to solve the above mileage puzzles. Calculators also help kids keep track of their spending money, sales taxes, and foreign currency exchanges. Or use it to play math or estimation games in the car (see Tip #47).

Thermometers (see Tip #19)

Binoculars

You need not purchase an expensive pair, since you want them in the clutch of small hands. But particularly on a nature trip, binoculars can add intricate details to your wildlife sightings.

Travel Tip 26

I'm Game

Commercial Travel Activities

- all ages
- all academic skills, depending on game

Geography, history, and travel games are abundant. Don't overlook commercial toys and games as teaching tools for your trip. World and U.S. puzzles are a good addition to any toy shelf. There are many quality games to choose from. Several early childhood development specialists and teachers recommend the following:

Board Games
Made for Trade, A Game of Early American Life, Aristoplay
State to State, Smethport
Hail to the Chief, a presidential-election game that builds knowledge of U.S. history and geography, Aristoplay
Name That State, Educational Insights
Where in the World/Time/USA is Carmen Sandiego board games, University Games
Passtimes, A Game of History, Edutainment

Electronic Games
GeoSafari makes many geography, history, and science games.

Travel Games
Roadtrip, a license-plate game and great for car travel, ToySense, Inc.
Mad Dash, Three Minutes Across America, ITOS Enterprises

Tangoes, Rex Games

Crazy Games, Price Stern and Sloan

USA Geography Jingo, Gary Grimm

Sterling Publishing Co. makes books of *Brain Teasers, Card Tricks, Word Tricks, Coin Tricks, Math and Logic Puzzles,* whodunit games, and many others.

Brainquest Games, Workman

Learning Works publishes thinking-skills books such as *What Do You Think?, What Would You Do?,* and *Think on Your Feet.*

Mad Libs, Price Stern Sloan (This has always been a favorite of my children. I think they learned about adverbs playing *Mad Libs.*)

Klutz Games makes an assortment of games which are suitable for car travel, including an excellent sticker book, a laminated foldout called "Glove Compartment Games," and *Back Seat Survival Kit* that offers a multitude of travel activities, games, and crafts.

The 50 Great States, Liza Schafer, Scholastic, is a wonderful, compact hands-on learning game.

Hip Hugger Games, Smethport

Binary Arts make an assortment of educational games that are easy to carry along.

Milton Bradley makes many travel games such as *Memory, Guess Who, Perfection, Connect Four,* and *Yahtzee.*

Parker Brothers makes *Sorry* and other travel games.

Pavilion makes travel games such as *Roll-a-Word, Seabattle, Bingo,* and *Inline.*

Pressman makes travel games such as *Mastermind* and *Othello.*

Activity Books and Kits

Anti-Coloring Books, Workman

Kids America, Workman

Pocketbook-size, inexpensive books by Dover Publications, Inc., include paper dolls, sticker books, mazes, stained glass, dot-to-dot, and many more.

AAA Travel Activity Book is a great car-activity book.

Geography Wizardry for Kids, Barrons, contains 150 challenging projects, experiments, and crafts for school-age children.

Travel Fun Activity Pack, DK Publishing, Inc., is full of games and activities to keep the backseat travelers occupied.

Dover Publications, 31 East Second Street, Mineola, N.Y., 11501 makes a variety of educational activity books relating to travel, animals, transportation, and many other topics.

Spizzirri Publishing, Inc., makes activity books about state birds, flowers, coloring books, and tapes.

Yo Sacramento, Will Cleveland and Mark Alvarez (Millbrook), includes trivia about each state capital and ways to remember the capitals.

There are inexpensive notepads of several sizes with outlines of a U.S map. Take some along for writing down license tags, drawing travel plans, locating state capitals, or jotting down notes.

Buy an inexpensive clipboard for each child before the trip. Let them decorate the boards with permanent markers. This is a great way to organize paper in the car for drawing, writing, and tracing.

Resource Tip:

Most of these commercial games and activities can be purchased at learning stores or on the Internet at www.edumart.com/theappletree/ or by calling the Apple Tree at 1-800-536-2753.

Web Resources

- **all ages**
- **computer, history, geography, and language arts skills**

Take a ride on the World Wide Web if you have access to the Internet. If you don't, visit your library for access. From Web sites to make your plane reservations to safe sites for your kids to travel electronically to faraway lands, the Web is full of travel information for you and your kids.

Great Web Sites:

Yahoo! at www.yahooligans.com has all kinds of kid travel information, including *Connected Traveler,* a travel magazine, on-line adventures, destinations, and activities for home and school curricula.

Berits Best Sites for Kids at db.cochran.com/ db_html:theoSearchPage.db is a list of best sites for children, including environment, history, science and math, space, and world travel.

National Geographic at www.nationalgeographic.com/ kids/ includes travel fun and games for kids, the *National Geographic World* magazine on-line, kids' networks, and much more.

MapQuest! at www.mapquest.com, a large consumer travel site, offers maps, driving directions, travel plans, and much more travel information.

KidsCom, www.kidscom.com, is a launchpad for cool kid locations around the world as it brings the world closer to you.

Interesting Places for Kids at www.starport.com/places/forKids/ is a compendium of links to sites and pages for kids on the World Wide Web, including educational travel information.

Canadians Kids Page at www.onramp.ca/cankids/107arch.htm includes lots of kids' sites from around the world.

The Apple Tree at www.edumart.com/theappletree/ has geography and history games and a large inventory of educational games and supplies. This is a great resource for parents and teachers. You can also order most of the commercial merchandise listed in this book from this Web site.

Disney at www.family.disney.com includes information about destinations, adventures, and travel advice.

The Global Online Adventure Learning Site at www.goals.com offers young explorers opportunities to travel on educational adventures.

At **http://www.indo.com/distance**, you can check your trip mileage. This Web site estimates the number of miles between cities.

At **travelwithkids.miningco.com** you will find a comprehensive travel site offering vacation ideas, great destinations, family travel links, and much more.

PART TWO

• •

Travel Wise

On the Road, In the Air, Once You're There.

The dog's been boarded, the final suitcase closed, and you're on your way. The kids are giddy with anticipation. At least for a while. Especially if you're traveling by car, it won't be long before you hear the familiar "How much longers?" and "Are we there yet?" No matter, like a dutiful Boy Scout, you're prepared! Here's what to do to get the best learning experience from your trip.

✏ Travel Tip 28

Postcard Gallery of Fun

- **all ages**
- **language arts skills**

The inexpensive but alluring postcard is ideal for many reading and writing projects.

Activities:

a) **Matching Memory Game.** Collect two each of twenty to thirty postcards at different stops through your trip. When you return home, cover the back of the postcard with a sheet of paper or index card cut to size. Make a matching/memory game from the postcards. Turn them over with the paper side facing up. The first player turns over two postcards, trying to get a match. The player who collects the most pairs wins the game. Extra points can be given if the child names what the postcard depicts. It's also a great way to jar your memory of fun vacation moments.

b) **Postcard Diary.** Encourage your child to write a daily, dated postcard about trip experiences, address it to herself, and mail it back home. When she arrives, she will have a written and pictorial record of her trip.

c) **Postcard Scribe.** Appoint your child as the family correspondent. Take along addresses of family and friends, and let your child select postcards to record the trip through a child's eyes.

d) **Postcard I Spy.** When you visit a museum, zoo, or

historical area, purchase several postcards in the gift shop depicting paintings, animals, buildings, or artifacts you might see during your visit. Have your child find the originals that match the postcard pictures as he walks through the exhibits. Let him keep the postcards and put them on a ring as a reminder of the outing or as a reference of museum offerings.

e) **Postcard Rings**. Throughout your trip, collect postcards with your child which might be of particular interest during a unit of study at school. For example, if you visit Alaska and you know that your second-grader has an upcoming study of the Iditarod, collect several cards pertaining to dog-sleds, Nome, Susan Butcher, and Alaskan huskies. Punch a hole in the corner, put them on a key ring, and you have a great resource for all the students. Your child will love to present her firsthand knowledge.

f) **Make Your Own Postcards**
supplies: blank postcards obtained at the post office, trip pictures, glue

Encourage your children to make their own postcards out of snapshots they took from their camera (Tips #58 and 59). They could also draw an illustration of their trip to send to family and friends as thank-you notes for hospitality, or to send to other friends and pen pals to share their trip. Glue a blank U.S. government postcard to the back of the picture, write your message in the space provided and mail it. Your children's friends will be especially delighted to see a friend featured on a postcard.

Travel Tip 29

Sign Language

- **early school age**
- **language arts skills**

Billboards and highway signs provide many opportunities for language arts and visual learning. We have played the letter game many times with my children where we start with *a* and find words beginning with all the letters in the alphabet as we pass highway signs. Unless there's a zoo nearby or you're passing through Vicksburg, some letters are hard to spot.

Other Sign Activities:

a) Give your children a list of common travel words such as *exit, motel, McDonald's,* and see whether they can match their list with signs along the way.

b) Play a word-association game. Your child picks a word from the first sign she spots and calls it out. Another player responds with the first word that comes to mind related to the first word. For example: She might call out *mile,* you might respond *car,* she might add *bike,* then you add *trail,* and she says *trees,* and so on. You can start another word after one minute or continue until you get tired.

Variation: play the same game, but use rhyming words.

Travel Tip 30

"Tell Me More, Tell Me More"

The Art of Storytelling

- **all ages**
- **language arts, creativity, and auditory skills**

Storytelling is perhaps the simplest tip of all. No supplies are needed but your memory and imagination. This is particularly fun if you're visiting family or places that trigger childhood memories. Children like nothing better than to hear about life when you were a child. You can tell stories straight from your childhood or embellish them and present them as fictional characters. My dad kept a line of "Three Boys Stories" going throughout my childhood. They were based on his and his two brothers' childhood fun growing up in small-town Oklahoma during the depression. Despite meager times, the "Three Boys Stories" were rollicking good yarns filled with sandlot baseball vignettes and practical jokes played on their unsuspecting mother. Although my dad never owned up to his own participation in the "Three Boys Stories," we children couldn't get enough of these "fictional" boys always on the prowl for fun. A friend told me about her dad's "Freddie the Frog" stories that he told to her and her brother and cousins. A long car trip is just the place to spin stories of your wild youth, and encourage your child to spin some of his own.

✎ Travel Tip 31

More Storytelling

- **all ages**
- **language arts and creativity skills**

Begin a group story. Select two characters, add a setting. Have your children add to the story. Ask questions to spur it along.

Variations:

a) Bag Story

Write the beginning of sentences or situations on several slips of paper. Put them in a bag and have your child draw a slip of paper and weave the sentence into a story. Examples: "When it snows, Frank can't wait to...." "If there is one thing that Sally won't eat, it's...." "You wouldn't believe what happened the first time Ashley tried to...." "Once upon a time, King Horatio decided to...."

b) Alphabet Story

Each sentence in the story must begin with the same letter. These stories will be short, but challenging. For example, "Samantha had a chore to do. She had to go to the store for her mother. Somewhere along the way, she ran into her best friend. Susan begged Samantha to come see her new puppy. 'Saturday was the best day of my life,' Susan said. 'Sasha came to live with us.' Samantha was so excited to see Susan's new puppy that she forgot all about going to the store. Suddenly she called her mom and told her she forgot what she was supposed to buy. 'Spinach,' said her Mom. 'Spinach!' replied Samantha. She now remembered why she had forgotten to go to the store!"

c) Puppet Story
supplies: old socks, lunch paper bags, crayons or markers, stickers

Turn your car or airplane ride into a puppet theater for impromptu stories to delight your youngest travelers. Young children love to make puppets and they're an easy take-along craft. Gather some mismatched socks (not a problem in our house) or lunch bags and silly-face stickers. Encourage your child to make up a puppet play. On an airplane, (unused) air-sickness bags can also be transformed into a puppet.

d) Favorite Story
Have your children retell a favorite or well-known story such as "The Three Bears." They can stay close to the original or embellish it to their hearts' content.

e) Packing Story
Start the game by saying "I'm going to Grandma's" (or New York, or camp out, or wherever you choose) "and I'm packing my teddy bear" (or toothbrush, toenail clippers, or whatever you want to pack). Each person adds something to the suitcase. But to put your item in the suitcase you must first list all the other items that have already been "packed." You can also play the game with the letters of the alphabet: "I'm packing an apple." "I'm packing an apple and a butterfly net." "I'm packing an apple, butterfly net, and a cap...."

✏ Travel Tip 32

Journalism 101

Trip Diaries

- all ages
- language arts skills

supplies: notebook or journal

Trip diaries can sharpen your child's observational skills along with writing skills. And no child is too young to begin a trip diary. Your preschooler probably can't write yet, so staple some construction paper together and have your youngster interpret her trip through pictures. You can write down her text under illustrations. Encourage older children to keep in their journal a daily record of the trip. Any writing sharpens writing skills, so the goal is simply to have them put words on paper. Younger children may have a goal of writing one line every day: June 8—"We rode in the car and saw cows and ate at McDonald's," June 9—"We got to Grandma's and she had a surprise for me."

Older children may want to include as much specific information as possible:

colors—perhaps a great sunset

details—number of miles covered in one day

feelings—"I've never been so hot in my whole life as when we took that walk through the desert trail. I wouldn't want to be a cactus plant."

reactions—"I knew mountains were tall, but I didn't know they were that tall!"

observations——"I never knew how many grain elevators I

could spot driving through small towns in Kansas."

humor—"When we arrived in New York, I'd never seen so many cars in my life and guess what, they're all yellow and say 'Taxi' on them."

dialogue—Mom said, "Will you please just stop at a gas station and ask directions?" Of course, Dad said, "So you think I'm lost, huh? Well, I know exactly where I am." And then Mom said, "Okay, then why are the Washington, D.C., signs backward on the other side of the interstate?"

• •

Book Resource Tip:

 Amelia Hits the Road, Marissa Moss (Tricycle). This kid-friendly book inspires young travel writers.

Travel Tip 33

Interactive Journal

- school age
- language arts skills

supplies: notebook and pencil

Help your child write a trip journal that talks back. Purchase any kind of notebook for him to keep a trip account, and when he makes a journal entry, add a response in the form of humor (a joke or riddle is always a kid pleaser), a question ("So with the purchase of your stuffed zebra, how much money do you have in your trip account?"), or a comment about his entry: "Yes, I really liked the candle-making shop in Williamsburg, too. Clothes sure have changed since colonial days, haven't they?" Encourage your child to draw illustrations in the journal. Even the youngest can draw a picture of what he saw at the National Zoo. Trip entries can be as simple as what they ate at Burger King or how many miles they traveled that day. If you respond to their creative process, they will keep writing.

. . . .

Highway Ribbery

What ten letter word starts with g-a-s?
Automobile
Why did the little boy in the backseat pull out paper and crayons?
The sign said 'drawbridge.'
When does a car get angry?
When it comes to a cross road.
What's the funniest car on the road
A jokes-wagon.

Joanne E. Bernstein and Paul Cohen,
Riddles to Take on Vacation

✎ Travel Tip 34

Road Poetry

- **school age**
- **language arts skills**

Children are natural poets. As they learn language, they

develop an ear for rhythms, cadences, and literary devices such as alliterations and metaphors. Because language is an emerging and exploding skill, children naturally organize words and images in patterns that may be unconventional. Let them experiment. Since travel is such a rich sensory experience, they should have much to draw on. Read poetry aloud to your children and ask them to listen to the rhythm and word choices. For this exercise, I highly recommend Jack Prelutsky's *Ride a Purple Pelican:*

Late one night in Kalamazoo
the baboons had a barbecue,
the kudos flew a green balloon,
the poodles yodeled to the moon....

Look for regional poems about your destination. In Alaska, I found a wonderfully whimsical poetry book, *Lucky Hares and Itchy Bears*, written by Susan Ewing with delightful illustrations by Evon Zerbetz, which features fifteen poems about Alaskan animals:

Sea Otter
Imagine munching urchins
While floating on your back
and smashing clams upon your chest—
It's WHAM, and then CUH-RACK!
For Otter it's not awkward
To snack or snooze afloat,
He bobs upon the ocean waves
Just like a furry boat.
And just like boats have anchors
To stay right where they are,

Otter
   Wraps
      Himself
         In Kelp
            To keep from drifting far.

After you've read poetry to your children, ask them to write down some images from their trip. After experimentation, clouds might be transformed from "fluffy white cotton" to "a snowshoe hare chasing after a snowball on a soft pillow." Encourage them to write circle poems, poems in the shape of a butterfly, fish, or mountain. Instead of *pretty, nice,* or *beautiful* suggest more descriptive words such as colors, shapes, or images. Suggest limericks, haikus, or free verse. Limericks have a rhyming pattern of *a-a-b-b-a-a* and are usually humorous. Ogden Nash was a master limerick writer:

The Panther
The panther is like a leopard
Except it hasn't been peppered,
Should you behold a panther crouch
Prepare to say Ouch.
Better yet, if called by a panther,
Don't anther.

The Rhinoceros
The Rhino is a homely beast,
For human eyes he's not a feast
But you and I will never know
Why nature chose to make him so.
Farewell, farewell, you old rhinoceros,
I'll stare at something less preposceros

Haikus are short three-line poems with a 5-7-5 syllable pattern and traditionally are written about aspects of nature:

Waterfall
The white waterfall
Splashing into the river
going way down stream

Michelle Bundren, age 11

Help them pick a subject from the trip (an animal they saw at the zoo, watching gulls at the beach, peering over the edge at Grand Canyon, standing under the St. Louis Arch and wondering how it was built). Don't wait to become a poet until after you arrive home. Compose in the car as you drive along. Pretend you're a cowboy on a long cattle drive. Use your imagination and draw on the wealth of images all around you.

Travel Tip 35

Tell It Like It Is

Audio Stories

- all ages
- language arts and history skills

supplies: tape recorder and blank audiotapes

Take a tape recorder on the trip to record songs, stories, and the day's events for an oral history of the trip. Record family stories as the miles roll by or record your children making up stories in the backseat, and amuse them by playing it back to them later, perhaps at home. Compose an oral letter to Grandpa along the way including anecdotes from your trip. As you visit friends and relatives, ask them about experiences when they were your children's age, and record their answers. What was their school like? Did they have pets? What were their hobbies? Record interesting sound effects along the way such as a train whistle, the noisy taxis in a big city, or animal sounds. Include movie, park, tour, or restaurant reviews. When you return home, make a pictorial to go along with your audiotape. Draw pictures of Grandpa's life on the farm or the thousands of taxis blowing their horns in New York City.

✎ Travel Tip 36

Trip Reporter

- school age
- language arts, geography, and organizational skills

If your family is going on an extended trip during the school year, perhaps on a sabbatical or work-related journey for several weeks, you will want to check with your child's teacher about keeping up with school curriculum during your child's absence. In our age of telecommunications, e-mail, and fax, there are many ways to continue the classroom education from far afield. Perhaps you can suggest that your child write a weekly newsletter or travel diary to send back to her classmates to inform them of the culture, geography, people, weather, language, and history of the places she is visiting. She can paste on or scan in photographs, postcards, and other trip memorabilia. Her classmates will look forward to her electronic correspondence as they travel vicariously with her. Also send the newsletter to family and friends who want to keep up with your travel. You may want to bring home souvenirs, such as foreign currency, reflective of your extended journey to share with your classmates. Why not choose a special book to donate to the school library to illuminate your travel experience for everyone?

Travel Tip 37

Window to the World

Window Play

- preschool, early school age
- language arts, math, and creativity skills

supplies: vinyl stickers such as Colorforms and vinyl sheets available at craft or learning shops.

Before you leave, cut shapes from the plastic sheets that will be useful for story building. Shapes might include houses, animals, balls, squares, rectangles, people, flowers, triangles, trees, cars, or letters. Children can build their own story scenes on the car or airplane windows or trays.

• •

Resource Tip:
Wikki Stix, which can be purchased at learning and toy shops, will make an additional fun story prop and easily will attach to windows and trays.

✎ Travel Tip 38

Tray Play

- • **preschool and early school age**
- • **memory and language arts skills**

supplies: cookie sheet or tray, bag of small objects: paper clip, key, rubber band, Cheerios, pencil, inexpensive jewelry, small toys collected from kids' restaurant meals, golf tee, crayon, battery, different size buttons.

Join your child in the backseat or let siblings play this game together. Set four or five small objects randomly on a tray and cover with a piece of paper or paper towel. Lift the covering and let your child look at the objects for a specified amount of time (perhaps fifteen to thirty seconds, depending on age and number of objects). An older child can keep time with a stopwatch. Cover the items and see how many objects your child can recall. Increase, decrease, and rearrange the objects each time. You can also use the objects to sort by size, color, function, and material.

• •

Resource Tip:

You can use a rectangular plastic container with a lid to store the objects, and the container can also be used as a tray.

✎ Travel Tip 39

Time Flies

Make a Trip Calendar

- all ages
- language arts, temporal, sequencing, and
  creativity skills

supplies: paper, markers and crayons, stickers

Make a trip calendar of events while traveling. It could be an extension of Tip #11. Since a child has little temporal concept, a calendar will provide a visual aid to help him understand the length of the trip and how many more days he will be traveling. And it's a good way to record daily activities. The calendar can be organized any way you like. Each day can be a page, or you can mark off a week on a legal-size sheet of paper. If you make it before you leave, you might laminate it and use markers to record events. Jot down animal sightings, museums you visited, places you ate, hotels you stayed in, and other notes. Add ticket stubs, stickers, and other memorabilia you pick up along the way to illustrate the calendar.

Monday	Tuesday	Wednesday	Thursday	Friday
Museum!	Baseball Day!	To the Beach!	Flew Kites at the Beach!	Saw a Jellyfish

Travel Tip 40

It's All Relative

Family History Trivia Game

- all ages
- family history and language arts skills

supplies: index cards for simple version; follow instructions in the book listed below for more structured games.

This new game takes *Trivial Pursuit* in a "relatively" new direction. The game can be played in the car, especially if you're visiting relatives, and can teach your child, at the same time, about famous and infamous incidents in your family history. Developed by two sisters, Lynn Bonsey and Lorna Healey, the game involves gathering trivia questions that only relatives might know about each other, such as "How did Susie lose her first tooth?" or "What was Aunt Mary's dog's name?" The game can be played individually, in teams or as a quiz contest. Each member of your family can brainstorm about family trivia and personal history, and write down ten (or as many as you can come up with) trivia questions on index cards. See how many questions family members can answer correctly.

To come up with questions, you might want to review photographs, diaries, and historical events in your family before you leave. The more you play the game, the more intricate your questions become. Along the way, as you tell your children about family history, more questions will come to mind. You can divide the game into categories: **Entertainment** (What was Susie's role in the class talent show?), **Sports** (What nickname did Joe's gym teacher give him?), **Statistics** (How much did David weigh when he was born?), and **Awards** (What place did Jeff get in the pinewood derby?). Keep a collection of questions and add to them as you visit relatives and learn more about your family heritage.

Resource Tip:

For a copy of Lynn Bonsey and Lorna Healey's book, *It's All Relative,* which includes reproduction game pieces and complete game rules, send $12.95 to RR1 Box 5095B, Toddy Pond Road, Surry, Maine 04684, or call (207) 667-2968.

✎ Travel Tip 41

News From Across the Country

- **school age**
- **language arts skills**

During occasional gas stops, purchase the local newspaper. It's amazing what you can learn about local culture from the newspaper, be it a city or hollow. I happened to be in New Orleans the week before Mardi Gras one year. The Sunday paper listed all the kings and queens, "Lords of Misrule," debutantes, and squires. I unexpectedly read the Living Section cover to cover because I found the French-based society names and lavish costumes so fascinating. Once when my kids and I were visiting "The Little Apple," Manhattan, Kansas, we read in the "crime" section of the newspaper that someone's lawn mower had been stolen out of his garage. Not only can you stay up on current events as you travel, but newspapers can be the best resource for learning about local culture and interesting people. Clip interesting articles which might be used for future reference or school projects.

✐ Travel Tip 42

Lights....Camera...Action!

Producing a Trip Video

- **school age**
- **language arts, creative, and visual skills**

supplies: video camera, pretend microphone (can be a flashlight), paper

So you want to be a movie star? If the Griswolds can do it, so can you. Make your own "Vacation" movie and let your children be the directors and/or cinematographers. Encourage them to write scripts as you travel. Include humor, local color, pertinent facts, and entertaining anecdotes. Their movie can be as original as their creative minds. They might want to interview local people such as museum docents, off-duty lifeguards at the beach, tour-bus drivers, souvenir-shop owners, relatives, and friends. They can make cards to hold up for the camera to introduce points of interest along the way. Using a microphone prop, they can be "trip reporters" on location while Mom or Dad videotapes. Don't forget the trip weather report and sports (from a major-league baseball game to frisbee on the beach). Include sound effects: the waves breaking on the beach, animal sounds, the noise and commotion of a big city. When you return, you can help them edit their production into a short feature for friends and family to view—and as a rainy-day event months later.

Travel Tip 43

License to Thrill

License Tag Games

- **school age**
- **math and language arts skills**

a) **The Updated License Plate Game**
If you've traveled by car, you've probably played the license plate game. It's always fun. In fact, we play it on almost every car trip. One child is the designated secretary and writes down all the state license tags that your family can spot. One year on a trip to Colorado, we found the license plates for forty-nine states (including Hawaii), but we just about gave up on Alaska. At a stoplight in Colorado Springs, there it was, the elusive tag on a pick up truck just in front of us. A cheer rang through the car and I was grateful for the native Alaskan, who was probably a student at the U.S. Air Force Academy.

b) **Vanity Plate Decoding**
supplies: index cards and pen
A fun variation of the game includes decoding vanity plates. Purchase a pack of index cards, and as cars pass, jot down the vanity plates. After you've collected about twenty,

play a game with your backseat passengers to see who can come up with the message first. Give your kids some cards and ask them to come up with their own vanity plates.

c) License Plate 21

Each player notes the tag number of different cars as they pass. Quickly add the tag numbers in your head or, for younger players, jot the numbers on paper and add. Who can get closest to twenty-one without going over? For young math whizzes, multiply the tag numbers and see who can find the highest number.

d) Design a Tag

Design a new license tag for your home state, the state you are visiting, or your family.

Travel Tip 44
Collect a State

- **preschool, early school age**
- **math skills**

supplies: yarn or plastic necklace cord, beads, pins, and small collectibles

Children love collections. At your local hobby shop, buy a plastic necklace cord and beads. Begin an add-a-state necklace. Whenever you pass through a new state, give your children a bead to add to their necklace. After the trip, put the trip necklace in a safe place and add to it on your next trip. You can also play this game by using pins on baseball caps or any small collectibles that can be easily acquired state by state. You can use the necklace to play several math games. Ask your children to count their beads/pins. Ask them to estimate how many they will have at the end of the trip. Beads are great to use for addition and subtraction skills: "You have four beads; if we drive through two more states, how many beads will you have when we get there?"

They can also count their different beads and graph them (see Tip #48).

Variation: Give each child a bead every 50 or 100 miles and have them estimate how many they will have at the end of the day or trip.

Travel Tip 45

Pennywise

Trip Budgeting

• school age
• math and organizational skills

Encouraging your child to manage some of his own money is an excellent way to promote math skills while also teaching the value of money. Give your child some discretionary spending money for the trip. In his travel journal, he can keep a personal expense log of his purchases and a running balance. His calculator may come in handy when figuring his balance. If you're not comfortable with your child carrying his own money, you can establish a debit system in which he keeps track of the amount of money you have in safekeeping for him. Let him make his own purchases, while reminding him to keep the sales receipts as a record of his expenses.

Prior to the trip, he may want to earn some extra spending money above any allowance or discretionary money by performing household chores, walking neighbors' dogs, or storing their mail or newspapers while they're away. He should keep a ledger of his trip savings so he can plan how much money he will have to spend. Or make a deal with him that you will match his earnings up to a point to encourage him to be industrious. Set up a vacation jar like the "Free Parking" square in Monopoly. Put loose change in it. Encourage your child to roll the money before you go on a trip and take him to a bank to exchange the change for some green stuff. We made a deal with our son once that he could pocket half of what he rolled from his father's overflowing change jar for the trip. We weren't aware of how many quarters were lodged among the pennies. He ended up rolling $50 worth of change and he was pretty proud of his $25 take.

* *

Resource Tip:

Another method of earning special vacation privileges might be through community service or volunteering. If your child has an upcoming class trip to Washington, D.C., or a Spanish-class excursion to Mexico City, suggest that she perform a certain number of hours of community service to "earn" her trip. It might be unrealistic to expect her to pay for the trip if she is not old enough to work legally. After all, you have to do a lot of household chores to pay for a plane ticket. But she can learn the value of volunteering as a way to help "pay" for her trip. My teenage neighbor helps coach a basketball team of underprivileged girls with his father. Several kids I know volunteer at the public library on summer afternoons. Habitat for Humanity is always in need of volunteers. The gift of time is an important value to teach, and when your child has an upcoming trip as incentive, she might be more willing to pull some weeds at a run-down house or visit a nursing home with cookies.

■ For volunteering ideas, check these inspirational books for kids: The *Big Help Book: 365 Ways You Can Make a Difference Volunteering*, Alan Goodman (Minstral), and *How Can You Help? Creative Volunteer Projects for Kids Who Care*, Linda Schwartz (The Learning Works).

✎ Travel Tip 46

Sense with Cents

Money Games

- school age
- math skills

Money can also be used for games and incentives for good behavior. Give your child a moneybag of small change. Have her sort the different coins. Can she add up the coins? How many dimes? Pennies? This can also be a great graphing game (see Tip #48) Take ten coins and arrange them in chronological order. Who has the oldest coin?

Moneybags

One mom told me she gave each of her three children a bag of 100 pennies at the beginning of a trip. Each time they were rude to a sibling, they had to give a penny to the offended sibling. With inflation, perhaps a bag of dimes might be more current. Whatever the bargaining chip, sibling spats might also take a vacation. The sibs are welcome to spend their loot at the end of the trip, and you can be sure they will use all their acquired math skills to count and compare results.

Menu Math

Collect menus from restaurants as you travel (most restaurants are willing to donate a menu), and play menu math with your backseat math whiz. From her collection of menus, order your meals, and she gets to add up the bill. Don't forget the tip. Her calculator might come in handy on this game, particularly if the front-seat customers are famished. Order several meals from different menus. Point out the differences in prices. Why are chicken nuggets $3.95 at one restaurant and $5.50 at another? This game will use not only her math skills, it will also help her understand how much it costs to eat out. The menus can be used as trip collectibles and to play "restaurant" after you return home.

• •

Resource Tip:

When visiting Washington, D.C., don't miss the excellent tour of the Bureau of Engraving and Printing. It gives new meaning to the adage "Money doesn't grow on trees." I'm certainly glad I don't have the job to eyeball each bill coming across the press to make sure it's accurate in every detail, but I'm glad someone does.

Travel Tip 47

Are We There Yet?

Estimation Games

- **school age**
- **math skills**

"When will we get there?" is perhaps the most common estimation game played on a trip. In fact, I've never really considered it a game, just a way for my bored kids to pester me. But it can be made into a game. Traveling is the perfect opportunity for many estimation games to shore up math skills.

Activities

a) A favorite of mine growing up: My dad would pick a hill on the horizon and we would estimate the distance. Pick any landmark on the horizon and ask your kids how many miles away it is and how long it will take to get there. Calculators and stopwatches come in handy. Really stump them by asking what direction it is. Stash a package of Skittles or Starburst and offer a reward for the best estimator. Make sure the youngest also gets a chance to be successful.

b) Keep a constant estimation game going through your trip. How much will the meal cost? If we're 50 miles from Hays, Kansas, what time will it be when we arrive? (Let them answer their own "Are we there yet?") How many white cars (incidentally, the most popular color) will we see within the next mile? Ten miles? If you're traveling at 1,000 feet above sea level, what's the altitude of the mountains up ahead? Highway signs and maps will often give this information. Airports also lend themselves to estimation games. How many people fit on the airplane? How many flights a day leave from the airport? Your particular day? How many people a day go through the airport? (Your ticket-counter attendant or information booth can answer some of these questions.) What will be the temperature at cruising altitude? Or have them estimate something that really interests them—how many M & Ms are in a package?

c) Exaggerate when you're asked "How much longer?" Say "By Christmas" or some other far-off date. Each time a backseat traveler inquires, shorten the time frame: "Thanksgiving," "Halloween," "Next week," "Tomorrow," "After lunch."

d) Plan ahead and take a bag of jelly beans, other candy pieces, or fish crackers, and let each child guess how many are in the package. Count and divide them evenly among your backseat charges.

. . . .

Resource Tip:

▆ *How Much Is a Million?*, David M. Schwartz (William Morrow), is a delightful look at number estimation.

. . . .

Fun Travel Fact

Dave Kunst left home in Wasica, Minn., on June 20, 1970, and returned on July 27, 1974—the first person to walk around the world. He traveled 14,452 miles, took 20 million steps, and wore out 21 pairs of shoes.

Source: *Guinness Record Breakers*, Karen Romano Young

✎ Travel Tip 48

Of Soccer Shoes and Bats

Graphing Skills

- **school age**
- **math skills**

supplies: lined paper and markers or crayons

I've always been impressed with the variety of games that math teachers use to make math fun. One day my second-grader was fumbling around in her closet gathering shoes. "So what's up?" I inquired. "We're graphing shoes tomorrow and I decided to take my soccer shoe." Graphing shoes? Yes, graphing is big in her class. Each child was to bring his or her favorite shoe so they could graph the selections according to style (tennis, sandal, hiking boots....) and color.

On grandparents' visitation day, parents and grandparents were asked to respond to one of five opinions about bats (were they helpful, just plain scary....) Our answers appeared on a graph to enhance their bat study unit. I never quite know what I'll be asked when I step into her classroom. But I do know that she's learning important math skills graphing soccer shoes and bats, and she thinks it's loads of fun.

Traveling offers many ways to teach graphing skills. Be creative. How many candy pieces of each color are there in a package? Count and sort them. Take a lined sheet of paper and let one line represent one color of candy pieces in the form of a bar graph. With a red marker, fill in the bar, counting the number of squares on the bar which represent the number of red pieces. Other graphing ideas? How many cars of certain colors can you spot over a ten-minute period? How many kinds of fast-food restaurants can you locate over the next fifteen miles? What kinds of animals can you see? There may be so many cows by the side of the road that your child will need to estimate and count ten per space. How many states start with each letter of the alphabet? How about capitals? If you're traveling by plane, take a survey. What is the final destination of those sitting around you? You can graph the answers by city or state. How long will the passengers be on their trip? Two days? Fourteen days? Use your imagination.

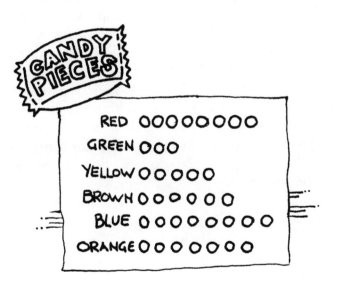

Travel Tip 49

Card Shark

Simple Card Games

- **all ages depending on the game**
- **math skills**

supplies: deck of cards and some imaginative "poker chips"

A simple deck of cards enhances many math skills and provides hours of fun. On our trip to Alaska, my children organized "blackjack" parties with other children on the trains and ferryboats. Their "poker chips" were Starbursts bought in the train gift shop. Even the youngest, with a little help, was able to add her cards quickly. The only hitch: At one point I overheard my teenage son admonish his little sister, "Hey, quit eating the poker chips. We won't have anything left to play with." Blackjack, or twenty-one, is a great math game. Each player is dealt two cards and the object is to see who can add a card getting closest to twenty-one without going over. Jack, queen, king are ten points, ace is one or eleven.

Other card games:

Double War: This game is played like War, but each player turns over two cards at one time. The winner of each round is the player whose cards add up to the most points, and that player gets to keep the cards. At the end of the game, the player with the most cards wins. As in War, jacks, queens and kings are worth ten points, aces eleven points, and jokers twelve points.

Solitaire: Take along a cookie sheet or tray (p
with sides to keep the cards contained) in the car for your
youngster to play solitaire.

Concentration: This game is great for visual recall. If you
play it with a full deck of cards, you will need a large playing
surface. You can modify the game for smaller surfaces,
however, and younger players by playing with just even or
odd numbers or one through nine. Turn the cards face down,
and each player turns over two cards, trying to match the
card rank (for example: two of hearts and two of diamonds).
If the cards match, the player keeps the cards. After all the
cards are matched, the player with the most card pairs wins
the game.

Commercial card games: Check your toy and learning
shop for cards games such as *Uno, Skip-Bo, BrainQuest, The
Ungame.*

* *

Book Resource Tip:
   The Book of Cards for Kids, Gail MacColl (Workman)
   Card Games for Children, Len Collins, Terry Carter, Bob
George (Barrons)

✏ Travel Tip 50

How Much Longer?

Distance Chain

- **preschool and early school age**
- **temporal, sequencing, and math skills**

supplies: constructions paper, scissors, and tape; or yarn piece, Cheerios, or beads

Give your child a visual aid to help her keep track of time and distance while traveling. Before you leave, help your child make any kind of a distance chain. Some suggestions include: a paper chain made with construction paper loops and tape, Cheerios chain, or large bead chain. Each loop or piece represents an increment of time or number of miles. For example, your child can remove a loop from her chain every thirty miles for a 300-mile trip, and toward the end of the journey, she can count the loops to help her understand how many miles she has gone. When she gets down to two loops she will be able to see that the trip is almost over without having to ask every mile, "Are we there yet?" If she uses beads or colored loops, she can sort them by color and count how many of each color she's removed.

Variation: Help your child write words that correspond to the trip (*river, ocean, Aunt Mary, Seattle,*) on the loops and, as she removes a loop, she can read the word to reinforce reading skills.

Fun Travel Fact:

A paper chain 40.67 miles long was made by students from the University of Missouri at Rolla. It had 450,000 links.

Source: *Guinness Record Breakers,* Karen Ramono Young

✎ Travel Tip 51

Two by Two

Number Game

- **all ages**
- **math skills**

The pair game is a simple and fun way to look at the world in number combinations. How many things can you name that come in pairs? Twins, shoes, mommy and daddy, ears and earrings, pant legs, hands on a clock, salt and pepper. Then move to threes: triplets, three blind mice, three men in a tub, number of cousins or siblings, apples, oranges and bananas, sides of a triangle. How about four: sides in a square, number of people who play tennis doubles, quadruplets, squares in the game, "foursquare," and so on. Find highway scenery to support your numbers. "Hey, there are four cows," "two red cars just passed us," "two grain elevators." One child can record the list and keep the game going throughout the trip as you see examples of number combinations.

✎ Travel Tip 52

All Over the Map

Geographic Place Names

- **school age**
- **geography and language arts skills**

I found a "weird and wonderful" atlas of the United States while browsing through a nature store one day. *All Over The Map* by David Jouris (Ten Speed Press) features thirty-three extraordinary U.S. theme maps which run the gamut from wacky to inspirational. The author divides his maps into categories and themes based on the names of towns around the country. The literary map identifies Thoreau, N.M., Lowell, Maine, and Twain, Calif. The sporting map denotes Rugby, N.D., Golf, Fla., and Matador, Texas. The Christmas map introduces Santa Claus, Ind., Christmas Valley, Ore., and Vixen, La., among many others. What a creative way to look at the country! I'll bet your children could come up with some great categories. Give them a U. S. map and see how many towns they can categorize by themes. How many towns beginning with *St.* can they find? How many towns have animal names? How about girls' or boys' names? As a footnote, I highly recommend Jouris' book. See how many of his mentioned towns you might pass through on your way. After all, it might be worth the effort just to say you've been to Toad Suck, Ark. Stop and take a picture by the road sign just in case your friends raise their eyebrows when you claim to have visited Monkeys Eyebrow, Ky.

Book Resource Tip:
🔖 Read *Cloudy With a Chance of Meatballs,* Judith Barrett (Atheneum) and have your child make up his own name for a town and a story about the people who live there.

• •

Greenwich was my hometown and a place to grow up. New York City is a place to grow up. Denver is a place to grow up. Orrville, Alabama, is a place to grow up and so is Thibodaux, Louisiana. These are all places where people are born, places where people die, and Greenwich was my place to be born and grow up. My problem was that I thought all towns in America were just like Greenwich.

Peter Jenkins, *A Walk Across America*

✎ Travel Tip 53

Flag It Down

- school age
- geography skills

Before you leave home, collect information about the states you'll be traveling through. What is the state flag and what do the flag's symbols represent? What is the flag's history? Ask an older child to search for some answers and explain to the rest of the family. What is the state flower and bird? On your trip, play a flag "I spy" game as you enter a new state. Who can spy the first flag? How many flags can you spy during your trek through the state? Collect small replicas of the state flags at gift shops and/or pennants of the region's sports teams or other regional mementos. As you drive along, have your children make their own flag on a piece of paper which represents them or your family. Can you spot the state bird? What does it look like? Or the state flower?

Once, in the finals of a school geography bee, my friend's son, who is an excellent geography student, lost on the question, "What is the state flower of Kansas?" Upon hearing of her schoolmate's unfortunate loss, my daughter piped up, "Oh that's easy, it's the sunflower." Her aunt and uncle from Kansas had given her a Kansas sunflower charm for Christmas. It pays to expose your child, however unintentionally, to all manner of geography trivia. You never know when it may come in handy.

Check out from the library a book on nautical flags and the messages they send. Create your own messages or design your own flags to signal the driver that it's time to eat, get gas, run, or find a motel.

• •

I am a fan of state flags. I like Maryland's gaudy flag, and Ohio's, and Arizona's, but Alaska's is my favorite. It's Ursa Major, the Big Dipper, in gold on a field of blue, with the lip of the dipper pointing, as it does in the sky, to Polaris, the North Star. The flag is brilliant in its simplicity, and unmistakable in its symbolism, and it's pretty. And it wasn't the idea of some professional designer. It was the idea of Benny Benson, who was the thirteen-year-old from Chignik, Alaska, when the Territorial Legislature adopted his design in 1927.

Charles Kuralt, *America*

✏ Travel Tip 54

Rubbing the Right Way

Artistic, Historic, and Nature Rubbings

- **all ages**
- **science, history, and creativity skills**

supplies: lightweight paper and crayons

Crayon rubbings are a great way to pass the time in the car or to bring history and nature home with you. Anything with texture such as car keys, earrings, and seashells can be used for rubbings. Tear off the paper from the crayons and your child can rub over plaques of historical buildings and statues, or names and dates on memorial markers. She can create seashell scenes from the beach using sand, paper and shells. On a nature hike, gather grasses, leaves, flowers, flat rocks, or fossils for a nature rubbing. See how many items you can find in the car to make rubbings, perhaps coins, trip memorabilia, and jewelry.

✎ Travel Tip 55

Play It Again, Kids

Reenactments

- **all ages**
- **history and geography skills**

My friend Debbie and her family travel more than anyone I know. Her husband is a sportscaster and hops a plane like most of us put keys in the ignition. Since her girls started school, she doesn't travel as much as she used to, but summers are a constant unpacking and repacking, off to ballparks around the country. Sounds glamorous, but she admits the constant travel gets tedious at times. Her solution? Seek out offbeat places for the kids to enjoy while Dad works. Once on a Philadelphia trip when they were visiting Independence Hall, they happened upon a historical reenactment featuring the fife and drum corps, patriots, and "Ben Franklin" leading a parade. She urged her daughters to participate and they ended up carrying flags of two of the thirteen colonies. The parade led to a square where Ben Franklin and a plantation owner began a heated debate on the issue of slavery. When you travel with an eye for adventure as she does, you never know what century you may end up in.

Another friend told me that she and her family enjoy Renaissance fairs that many communities hold to commemorate and reenact the medieval days. She said that they visited a fair in Norman, Okla., that featured period costumes, jousting knights on horses ,and an open-air market with all kinds of booths. At the time, her four-year-old daughter was mesmerized by princesses and fairy tales, so she bought her a magic wand. The wand became something of a disappointment when she pointed to a nearby tree, chanted a spell, and nothing happened. Her fairy-tale reenactment hadn't had enough fairy dust behind it.

When my son was a Cub Scout, his scout leader took the den to a Civil War reenactment in Arkansas. He came home full of stories and with a Civil War wooden gun replica that shot rubber bands. (As I recall, the gun didn't last too long after he used his sisters for target practice.)

Many areas of the country host reenactments of historical events. Probably the most popular occur in Williamsburg, Va., where children can visit cabinetmakers and blacksmith shops, as well as see the fife and drum corps. Children love reenactments, and perhaps you can borrow some of what you've learned to add to their school curriculum. In April, many schools in Oklahoma reenact the 1889 Oklahoma land run. Children dress in period clothing and carry ropes and stakes. When the gun goes off, they tear across the playground to claim their property. The reenactment might include a picnic lunch on their homestead. What better way to teach history than to reenact it? State historical societies can provide information on reenactments.

● ●

Book Resource Tip:

For comprehensive resources featuring Civil War reenactments, battlefields, monuments, and other Civil War information, check *The Civil War Trust's Official Guidebook to the Civil War Discovery Trail,* by the Civil War Trust, or *The Civil War Sourcebook: A Traveler's Guide,* by Chuck Lawliss (Harmony).

Travel Tip 56

"We the People"

A Behind the Scenes Look at Washington, D.C.

- school age
- history and social studies skills

Your senator or representative's office can be very helpful in planning a trip to Washington, D.C. Call your congressional representative's office to obtain free passes for VIP tours of the White House, Bureau of Engraving and Printing, FBI, State Department, Archives, National Cathedral, Mount Vernon, John F. Kennedy Performing Arts Center, Library of Congress, Supreme Court, and U.S. Capitol. The VIP passes allow more extensive tours in smaller groups than tours open to the general public. Please be advised that each congressional member gets very few VIP passes and they're usually spoken for well in advance. Call and reserve yours as soon as possible, preferably several months in advance.

See Congress in action during a visit to the upper gallery at the U.S. Capitol. Passes to the gallery may also be obtained by your senator or representative. If Congress is in session, depending on the business being conducted, you can watch as bills are introduced and debated, and witness the roll-call voting system. Visit both the Senate and House galleries for a very different perspective on the government process. See how many Senators and Representatives you can recognize. Turn on *C-Span* in the evening for a perspective of what you saw "live." No history book can give your child such an experience. You can almost feel the decades of congressional debates echoing through the chambers.

If Washington, D.C., is not in your travel plans, how about your own state capitol? Call your capitol for tours and opportunities to watch your legislature in action (for teenagers see Tip #97). Often governors' mansions offer tours during certain times of the year. Your legislator can provide information about the best way to see your state capitol.

✐ Travel Tip 57

Home Sweet Home

Historical Homes

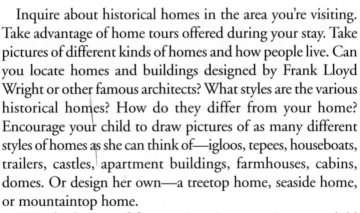

- **school age**
- **science, history, and creative skills**

Inquire about historical homes in the area you're visiting. Take advantage of home tours offered during your stay. Take pictures of different kinds of homes and how people live. Can you locate homes and buildings designed by Frank Lloyd Wright or other famous architects? What styles are the various historical homes? How do they differ from your home? Encourage your child to draw pictures of as many different styles of homes as she can think of—igloos, tepees, houseboats, trailers, castles, apartment buildings, farmhouses, cabins, domes. Or design her own—a treetop home, seaside home, or mountaintop home.

Visit the homes of famous Americans to give your child perspective about how children grew up in other centuries. See how Betsy Ross sewed her flag just off a busy Philadelphia street, or how small the cabin is that inspired Laura Ingalls Wilder's prairie stories. You think of Ulysses S. Grant as the great Union general and U.S. President. Did you know he had a farm that is now in the middle of St. Louis? Grant's Farm, run by the Busch family, offers wonderful tours. Seek out historic homes to add rich perspective of early American lifestyles.

● ●

Book Resource Tips:

Frank Lloyd Wright for Kids, Kathleen Thorne-Thomsen (Chicago Review)

The House That I Live In: At Home in America, Isador Seltzer (Macmillan)

Under Every Roof: A Kid's Style and Field Guide to the Architecture of American Houses, Patricia Brown Glenn (Preservation Press)

● ●

Fun Travel Facts

Top 10 Historic Houses in the United States (by number of annual visitors)
1. Graceland, Memphis, Tenn.
2. Isabella Stewart Gardner Museum, Boston, Mass.
3. Gallier House Museum, New Orleans, La.
4. Bonnet House, Fort Lauderdale, Fla.
5. Falling Water, Mill Run, Pa.
6. Victoria Mansion, Portland, Maine
7. Melrose, Natchez, Miss.
8. Bayou Bend, Houston, Texas
9. Olana, Hudson, N.Y.
10. Gamble House, Pasadena, Calif.

Source: *The Top Ten of Everything,* Russell Ash

✎ Travel Tip 58

Say Cheese, Please!

Trip Photographer

- school age
- creativity, language arts, and organizational skills

Buy each child a disposable camera and/or waterproof camera. Let him or her be the trip photographer along the way. You might suggest themes such as animals; views from hotel windows; skyscrapers; friends and relatives; lakes, rivers, oceans, and the wildlife that inhabits each; modes of transportation; or sporting events. Juvenile shutterbugs will have endless fun orchestrating their "photo shoots" by sneaking up on unsuspecting mallards swimming in a lake, or siblings swinging from a rope. They can snap one of the airplane cockpit or their sister's underwater somersault. Each photo is an expression of their imagination and creativity.

Teach your enthusiastic photographers about the fine art of photography. Show them some photographic books, particularly from the region you'll be visiting. Initially they may want to take pictures of everything they see. Encourage them to create a story with their pictures around their chosen themes. Explain that morning and late afternoon light is best for picture taking because there are better shadows when the sun is lower on the horizon. Seek out art galleries and museums which display photography.

My teenage son has developed an intense interest in photography and took a summer class in which he learned to develop his own film as well as more advanced photography techniques. On a recent trip to Aspen, Colo., we happened upon a photography exhibit at the Aspen Art Museum. My son, who groans at any mention of art galleries or museums, was pushing me through the door to view the exhibit and ended up leading the tour, explaining lighting and other techniques. I have supported and lauded his photography hobby, but now my biggest problem is affording all his trip film and development.

After you return from your trip, help your child make a picture scrapbook. The scrapbook can be made by stapling several sheets of construction paper together, or a sturdier scrapbook can be purchased. To ensure lasting memories, select acid-free paper and scrapbooks offered by companies such as Creative Memories, P. O. Box 1839 St, Cloud, Minn. 56302. In fact, there are many scrapbook accessories available such as stickers, cut outs, acid-free pins, special rulers, and scissors, to make his scrapbook a creative masterpiece.

If he has chosen a theme to photograph, such as trip animals, he may want to research more about the animals, add some captions, and present his work during an appropriate school unit. A younger child can dictate information for you to write and may need some prompting to remember details.

✏ Travel Tip 59

A Len's Eye View

- **school age**
- **science and creativity skills**

Encourage your child to snap a picture out of his hotel window. From this bird's-eye view, he can see buildings, landscapes, and the way cities are organized. Keep a diary of what's outside each window, and it will be surprising how many memories it will stir. Include pictures taken from windows of interesting structures: the Empire State Building, the Washington Monument, the Arch in St. Louis. Also take pictures of interesting architecture—buildings, fountains, monuments, sculptures. You may have seen framed pictures of distinctive doors in various cities. Similarly, frame some of your most interesting shots taken from windows which best capture the spirit of the city.

Pictures snapped from airplane windows upon approach to the runway can also capture a panorama of the city. Each city has a skyline personality as jagged buildings which look like giant building blocks from above jut up toward the sky. One mom recalled an incident when her family was flying into San Diego one sunny afternoon with the city spread below them. She pointed out to her children the large Coronado Bridge beneath them, and her small daughter replied, "I thought the main bridge was in San Francisco."

• •

Over the great bridge, with the sunlight through the girders making a constant flicker upon the moving cars, with the city rising up across the river in the white heaps and sugar lumps all built with a wish out of non-olfactory money. The city seen from the Queensboro Bridge is always the city seen for the first time, in its first wild promise of all the mystery and the beauty in the world.

F. Scott Fitzgerald, *The Great Gatsby*

✎ Travel Tip 60
Architecturally Speaking

- **school age**
- **science and artistic skills**

Seek out homes and buildings registered on the National Register of Historic Places. Contact your local historical society or National Park Service about sites which figure in our nation's history. The Congress of Art Deco Societies in Boston or the Los Angeles or Miami Art Deco Societies are excellent references to unusual art deco architecture so popular during the early part of the twentieth century. Point out different architectural features such as Greek columns, gargoyles, plantation homes, dormers, gables, eaves, domes, and arches to familiarize your child with different kinds of architecture. Point out styles that you find particularly appealing.

• •

Book Resource Tip:
For Children
> *Architects Make ZigZags: Looking at Architecture from A to*

Z, Roxie Munro (Preservation Press).

Architecture Counts, Michael J. Crosbie, Steve Rosenthal (Preservation Press), series of four books to introduce preschoolers to architecture

For Adults

For a guide to national historical properties, which features 62,000 places, check the *National Register of Historic Places 1966 to 1994,* National Park Service. This is a hefty book in bulk and price, so it's best reviewed at the library.

● ●

Steel, glass, tile, concrete will be the materials of the skyscrapers. Crammed on the narrow island the millionwindowed buildings will jut glittering, pyramid on pyramid like the white cloudhead above a thunderstorm.

John Dos Passos, *Manhattan Transfer*

✎ Travel Tip 61

The Art of the Matter

Museum Adventures

- **all ages**
- **creativity and artistic skills**

Art appreciation can begin as early as preschool. After all, you don't have to be able to read to view a painting or notice the way colors interact. If you cross paths with an art museum along your route, don't hesitate to introduce even your youngest children to the fascinating world of art. Most likely your child already thinks of himself as an artist, and well he should. All of those kindergarten masterpieces attached to your refrigerator door validate his opinion of himself. Art has so much relevance to children that taking his artistic education one step farther by introducing him to galleries, museums, and displays may spark an even greater artistic self-expression and confidence. Do keep in mind attention span and wiggle quotas, so you don't end up frustrated by young children's inability to focus and be quiet.

Introduce your school-age children to artists from the region you are visiting, or artists whose works may be showing at local museums and galleries. It's hard to visit Santa Fe, N.M., without seeing Georgia O'Keeffe's bright, vibrant images of nature. Likewise, Andrew Wyeth and his portraits of American life in parts of the Northeast. As you explore the world of art, point out the different kinds of art. You don't have to get too technical to explain the difference between an impressionist painting and an abstract painting. Your child's eyes can be very discerning. As you visit museums and galleries, play the scavenger-hunt postcard game (Tip #28). Or go on an "I spy" treasure hunt to see how many circles, squares, animals, trees, people, food, flowers, or cars he can find in the artwork. Visit the museum gift shop. He may want to purchase an inexpensive book about his favorite artist or choose some postcards of paintings to share with his art class. After his visit, he may want to draw a picture in his personal style or imitate in his trip journal a favorite artist's style. Encourage him to draw a self-portrait. As you drive along, point out artists' styles on billboards and other advertising venues. The graphic arts are all around us. Point out examples and let your young artist put pencil to paper.

• •

Resource Tips:

Visiting the Art Museum, Laurene Krasny Brown and Marc Brown (Unicorn)

◆ *Looking at Pictures: An Introduction to Art for Young People,* Joy Richardson (Harry N. Abrams)

At Chagall for Children, a new exhibit at the Kohl Children's Museum in Wilmette, Ill., near Chicago, children can create their own artwork imitating Chagall's unusual style.

✏ Travel Tip 62

Think Green

Learning About Ecology

- **all ages**
- **science and value skills**

Kids are eager to do their part in preserving planet Earth. They just need some direction and encouragement. Have you ever been driving down the highway when someone in a car beside you throws a cigarette butt or cup out the window and your children chant in unison, "Litterbug, litterbug"? You probably don't want to squelch their contempt. Children learn lifelong habits at an early age, and protecting and preserving the beauty of our land can make a difference for generations.

One mom told me that she and her daughter witnessed a litterbug who threw a cigarette box out the car window, followed by a cigarette butt. She had just learned of a litter hot line in her state, so her eight-year-old daughter wrote down the litterbug's license-tag number. When they arrived home, they called the litter hot line and reported the incident. The hot-line attendant told them that they would send an appropriate warning letter to the offender. She said the incident truly impressed her daughter.

Activities:
a) Take along some extra trash sacks to pick up a few trash items along the beach, roadside, rest stops, motels, and parks. If every citizen picked up one piece of outdoor trash every day, that would deposit over 200 million pieces of trash. If

each piece averaged one ounce, that's about 7,000 tons of trash collected daily. Wouldn't our land look pristine?

b) Refill water bottles in drinking fountains and sinks rather than buying new bottles at every stop.

c) Ask for paper cups and plates rather than Styrofoam, and explain why to your kids. Tell them that Styrofoam will be in our garbage dumps forever because it will not break down. It' s also a danger to animals because they think it's food. All those "happy meal" containers won't look too happy when the next generation digs them up.

d) Along the way, ask where recycling bins are located to recycle your glass and cans.

e) It sure seems simple, but it makes a difference. Make sure the lights are off in your hotel when you leave and the thermostat is turned to low or off.

f) Go out of your way to point out pollution and other ecological problems. You only have to visit a polluted beach to see the contrast between Mother Nature at her finest and man at his worst. When the beautiful whitecaps break and fall on a beach of sludge, you don't exactly want to spend the day sunning and dipping. When our family visited Alaska, we went on a fine tour of the Port of Valdez. I was in awe of the men and women who brilliantly engineered the Alyeska Pipeline Project, which supplies a quarter of our domestic oil. Also prominently displayed was a rendering of the 1989 oil spill that wreaked such havoc on the fragile ecosystems of Prince William Sound. I felt that the oil spill was as important a lesson for my children as the phenomenal engineering feats of the pipeline.

Resource Tip:

50 Simple Things Kids Can Do To Save The Earth, The Earthworks Group

Going Green: A Kid's Handbook to Saving the Planet, John Elkington, Julia Hailes, Douglas Hill, and Joel Makower (Demko Media)

Not–So–Fun Travel Facts

- Americans throw away 25 billion Styrofoam coffee cups every year and 2.5 million plastic beverage bottles every hour.
- Americans throw away enough glass bottles and jars to fill the 1,350-foot twin towers of New York's World Trade Center every two weeks.
- If all the cars on the U.S. roads had properly inflated tires, it would save nearly 2 billion gallons of gas a year.

Source: *Going Green*

✎ Travel Tip 63

Gather Ye Roses

Nature Fun

- **all ages**
- **creativity and science skills**

Nature provides her own splendor on camping and

outdoor trips. These are some fun activities to do in the wild, or after you return home with your nature artifacts.

a) Nature Place Mats
supplies: construction paper, clear contact paper.

Gather seeds, berries, flowers, grasses around the camp and trail sites. Make sure the plants are not legally protected. There may be plenty of artifacts to be gathered which have fallen to the ground. Glue them on a piece of construction paper. Older children can identify the plants from a field guide. Preserve them between two sheets of clear contact paper.

b) Outdoor Scavenger Hunt

Give your children a list of commonly found items in the area you're visiting. The children can collect them or simply note that they have found the item, since many wildflowers are rare and protected species and should be left undisturbed. Suggestions: pinecones, pine needles, dandelions, acorn, pods, birds (whatever kind are found in the area), walkingstick, moss, worm, butterfly.

c) Flower Pressing
supplies: large book, blotting paper, newspaper, nature artifacts

Gather nonprotected flowers, leaves, and other flat nature findings to make flower-pressed cards, bookmarks, and pictures when you return home. Store them carefully in labeled containers so they will not be damaged during your trip home.
1. Arrange the flowers and nature artifacts on the blotting paper.
2. Cover the artifacts with more blotting paper and newspaper. Put the artifacts and blotting paper between two heavy

books and store for four to six weeks.

3. Once the nature artifacts are dried, you can make pictures, cards, and bookmarks by gluing them on paper or cardboard. You may want to laminate them carefully or put clear contact paper over your dried picture.

d) Stained Glass Nature Picture

supplies: flat nature artifacts such as leaves, grasses, petals, seeds; waxed paper, iron, glue, newspaper or cloth, colorful one inch strips of paper (such as construction paper)

1. Arrange your nature artifacts between two pieces of wax paper.
2. Place newspaper or cloth over the waxed paper and press. As the waxed paper melts, it will seal the papers together.
3. Cut the edges to the desired size and glue the paper strips along the edges to make a frame.

Place your nature stained-glass window in a windowsill to catch the sunlight.

✎ Travel Tip 64

Call of the Wild

Nature Sightings

- **all ages**
- **science skills**

Along many scenic routes, you can discover bluebird trails, beaver dams, fossils, monarch butterflies, deer, and many other varieties of wildlife that may be new to your children.

Read about the local wildlife in a museum, gift shop, library, or nature store so you can be on the lookout for the natural habitats of animals. Bluebird nesting boxes can be found along many trails. They are small wooden boxes mounted on poles with a hole about one inch in diameter in the front of the box. While the boxes themselves should be left alone lest the shy bluebird abandon its nest, the boxes' presence should signal the possibility of a bluebird sighting in the area. Purple-martin houses can also be found along many wildlife trails. On a hike in Alaska, we happened upon a family of beavers beavering away building dams. My children unobtrusively stood back from the shore, transfixed by the natural wonder unfolding before them. Even the ubiquitous chipmunk on mountain slopes can engage a child's curiosity. Offer them opportunities to explore natural habitats, and at the same time teach them respect for the wilderness.

Learn how to call a bird and other animals. Wildlife responds by mimicking their sounds. Encourage your child to get up close to nature. Look for animal tracks. Can you identify the animal which left its signature print?

Perhaps the best way to learn about nature is to spend unstructured time puttering through woods and fields turning over logs, gathering worms, shuffling through leaves, poking around with a stick, playing hide-and-seek among the trees, and just being outdoors in the world's greatest natural laboratory.

Some great props for nature exploring are butterfly nets, jars with holes punched through the lids to catch insects, binoculars, field guides, and don't forget the insect repellent to keep away some less than desirable critters.

My friend Debbie, whose husband is a sportscaster, tells of the time she spotted some cardinals lurking around their new backyard bird feeder. She called her four-year-old daughter to the window to show her the ruby-red birds. Her daughter responded, "Cardinals? I thought they all lived in St. Louis."

Resource Tip:

Birdwatching for All Ages: Activities for Children and Adults, Jorie Hunken (Globe Pequot), teaches kids how to imitate, identify, and draw birds, and other activities to engage your young ornithologist.

Check your library for field guides that show pictures and offer information about the wide variety of species that may be crossing your path.

Animal Tracker, Jim Arnosky (Random House)

Animal Tracks and Traces, Kathleen V. Kudlinski (Franklin Watts)

* *

Travel Quote:

Earth hums. Put your ear to the ground and you might hear it, or the padding of paws, pounding of hooves, or faint brush of wings.

Geneen Marie Haugen, "Wild Sentries," from
Alaska Passages, edited by Susan Fox Rogers

✎ Travel Tip 65

Nature Diary

- **school age**
- **science and language arts skills**

supplies: notebook and colored pencils

On your outdoor trip to the mountains or woods, encourage your child to keep a nature journal. Each day she can record the wildlife that she saw, along with interesting plants and vegetation. Take a field guide to identify plants. Perhaps gather some seeds for your trip garden (see Tip #93). In a journal, your child can draw pictures of the wildflowers and insects she saw buzzing by. Find a good wildlife search spot on your trip. You might take along some wild birdseed to attract some varieties of birds. Take a stick to poke around plants and under vegetation. What can you unearth? Be careful to disrupt the habitat as little as possible. Remind your child that she is a guest in nature's home.

Sketch birds or other animals you see. For older kids, there are many step-by-step animal drawing books that you can purchase for the trip. Before you leave your site, see Tip #62 and take along a sack to pick up litter so the spot will be left a better place.

• •

Fun Travel Facts

Most-visited National Parks
  1. Great Smoky Mountains National Park, N. C./Tenn.

2. Grand Canyon National Park, Ariz.
3. Yosemite National Park, Calif.
4. Yellowstone National Park, Wyo.
5. Rocky Mountains, Colo.
6. Olympic National Park, Wash.
7. Acadia National Park, Maine
8. Grand Teton National Park, Wyo.
9. Mammoth Cave, Ky.
10. Zion National Park, Utah

Source: *The Top 10 of Everything*, Russell Ash

✎ Travel Tip 66

Digging in the Dirt

- school age
- science skills

Archaeology and *anthropology* are awfully big words for children. But if you explain it as digging in the dirt to find treasures, you might find some willing participants. Why not take your child on an archaeological dig to unearth some prehistoric artifacts? Your local anthropology or archaeology society can tell you about digs in your state that would be appropriate for the whole family. Often, sites are excavated before a construction project begins. After a survey of the ecosystem and surface, archaeologists determine whether the site may have had prehistoric activity.

Recently in Tulsa, an oil mansion needed a new driveway. Archaeologists excavated the area before the new driveway was poured and found historical artifacts which otherwise would have been buried under concrete. Many sites are not appropriate for children, but often these societies will have digs appropriate for the whole family. The Internet and the National Park Service also have information about archaeological digs that might be of interest.

Perhaps panning for a few gold flakes might spark a modern-day gold seeker. In towns along the Klondike Gold Rush Trail such as Fairbanks, Alaska, and around towns near the Sierra Nevada in California, treasure hunters can retrace the steps of the early-day gold diggers and try their own luck in gold panning. The take may not pay for the experience, but it's a great way to reenact the frenzy of the gold-rush days.

When you return home, stage your own dig. A friend told me she found some great cow bones in a field at a grandparent's farm. Her young children loved weighing, measuring, and studying the bones under a magnifying glass. After their experiments were over, they buried the bones in their sandbox for further finds.

• •

Book Resource Tip:
  Klondike Fever—The Famous Gold Rush of 1889, Michael Cooper (Clarion)

• •

History, geography, and imagination all converge at the frontier, which continues to speak to our distinctly American fascination with what lies on the other side of civilization—to our New World temptation to recreate ourselves in unknown territory. In some ways, the imperatives of the frontier haven't changed since the California gold rush or, for that matter, since Plymouth Rock.
  Jennifer Brice, "Dead Fish and Dreams," from
  Alaska Passages, edited by Susan Fox Rogers

✏ Travel Tip 67

Exploring Rivers and Streams

- **all ages**
- **science skills**

Explore the habitat of fields and streams. Buy a small aquarium for your child to tend at home with snails and fish. Let your child run the hose in the sandbox and set up dams, tunnels, and water channels. It's messy, but no better fun is available.

Activities:

a) Bring along some dried bread to feed ducks and geese.

b) Rent a sailboat and use the experience to talk about wind, currents, waves, and direction (tell them to keep their compass handy).

c) Ask around about a guide who can take you on a fishing trip. Whether you intend to catch pike in a Minnesota lake, bass in Missouri, or trout in a mountain stream, you will find guides very experienced in taking your family on a safe, productive fishing expedition. I have a friend whose favorite sport is fishing, and she has decorated her house in a fishing motif (complete with a fishing Santa yard decoration at Christmas). She and her family have traveled all over the country doing sport fishing.

d) When I was in the sixth grade, we hunted for crawdads on the last day of school. It was a tradition at my elementary school, a last chance at childhood before we headed to junior high. We brought bacon, string, a stick, a collection jar, and headed for a shallow stream by the school. My friend told me about the time she collected several jars of snails at a state park. Let your kids try their hand at capturing critters. Take along some jars with holes punched in their lids to collect small creatures. You might institute the "24-hour" rule. Your child can keep the creatures for 24 hours before returning them to their natural habitat.

e) Build a water scope to get up close and personal with the critters and plant life that inhabit marshes and streams.
supplies: a tall plastic container such as a sour cream or yogurt container, clear plastic wrap, rubber band, knife.

1. Cut off the bottom of the container and place the plastic wrap across, securing it with a rubber band to make it as watertight as possible.
2. Put the water scope with the plastic end down into the water at a stream or pond edge.
3. What kind of water life can you see? Use your water scope around grasses and lily pads. What amphibians might be lurking around the water's surface? Can you catch some tadpoles?

f) If fishing gets frustrating when the big one and all the little ones get away, you can still get up close and personal with fish at a fish hatchery, where you can learn about life cycle, feeding habits, and where they fall on the food chain.
My friend who loves to fish recalled a vacation experience when a hatchery dam broke and young fish poured into the stream. She said fishermen were shoulder to shoulder, pulling out multitudes of fish, as she and her children joined the fray. It wasn't long before the game warden appeared and

slowed the fishing free-for-all, explaining to the children that overfishing would deplete the stream of fish. She said it was a great lesson for her children about abiding by the rules that protect wildlife.

• •

Book Resource Tip:
🔖 *Kid's Incredible Fishing Stories,* Shaun Morey.

• •

I never string up a trout rod without wild anticipation. Often, I've been exhausted on trout streams, uncomfortable, wet, cold, briar-scarred, sunburned, mosquito-bitten, but never, with a fly rod in my hand, have I been unhappy. I can't express the joy I felt in my Montana September, driving slowly along a different river day after day, free of all obligations and open to all possibilities, with my fishing bag in the passenger seat beside me.

Charles Kuralt, *America*

Travel Tip 68

Cloud Cover

- all ages
- science and observation skills

Look overhead. It's a bird, it's a plane, no, it's an elephant. To a child, clouds can be fluffy white cotton candy or many varieties of animals. As you drive along, ask your children what they see in the clouds. Create a story about the overhead theater. It's amazing what fluffy-cloud stories spring from young, imaginative minds.

While you're gazing overhead, take cloud study one step farther. Explain that clouds are both predictors and causes of weather patterns. Teach your children the difference among cirrus, cumulus, and stratus clouds, and the weather associated with each.

Cirrus: High clouds made of ice crystals, they are wispy sheets of clouds known as "mare's tails." They usually indicate fair weather.

Cumulus: Piled-up masses of fluffy white clouds that often bring moisture. They are described as "cauliflowers."

Stratus: Low, gray clouds that usually look like a sheet. These clouds often bring fog, drizzle, or snow.

As you travel, can you recognize the kinds of clouds and what kind of weather they bring? As your plane ascends, point out the different kinds of clouds you can see through your window.

The best cloud lesson my family has experienced occurred when we were observing the famous Haleakala Volcano at sunrise on Maui—an island tradition. As masses of moist air, warmed by the first rays of sunlight, poured into the crater and converged with the cold nighttime air, the temperature inversion caused carpets of cumulus clouds to form before our eyes. It was a spectacular sight and a great condition for rainbows.

● ●

Clouds

White sheep, white sheep
On a blue hill,
When the wind stops
You all stand still.
When the wind blows
You walk away slow.
White sheep, white sheep,
Where did you go?

Christina G. Rossetti

A white cloud floated like a swan
high above Saskatchewan
the cloud turned gray at ten past noon,
it rained all day in Saskatoon

Jack Prelutsky, *Ride a Purple Pelican*

● ●

Book Resource Tip:
It Looked Like Spilt Milk, Charles G. Shaw (HarperCollins), a delightful preschool book exploring the many possibilities of cloud shapes.

Travel Tip 69
Rock and Stroll

- all ages
- science, geography, and creativity skills

Rocks hold a special fascination for children, and this curiosity can lead to discussions of geology and geography. Go on a nature walk and collect rocks and stones. Find a special rock to take home. What kind is it? Is it indigenous to the area? Can you find a fossil? Explain that fossils are molds that have been etched into rocks of plants and animals which lived millions of years ago.

Several years ago, when I was teaching a fifth-grade church class, to emphasize a biblical principle, I invited the class to bring their rock collections to share. To my amazement, one student had collected and categorized dozens of rocks from all over the world, and she was able to help other students classify their rocks. Her knowledge of geology was far superior to mine, and she told me she had developed a special interest in rocks while traveling.

Craft Activities:
a) Rock Painting
supplies: rock, paint, and paintbrush

Like clouds, you can often see pictures in rocks, and like snowflakes, no two are alike. Have your child search for a rock that suggests a picture to them. A flat rock with a curved top might be a turtle. A round rock might lend itself to a jack-o'-lantern. A tall rock might suggest a two-story home. Let their imaginations fly.

b) Rock Sculptures
Supplies: rocks, glue and paint (optional)
Gather rocks along a trail and build a rock community.
You can mark a trail as pioneers used to do with your rock
sculpture. Bring back your rock collection from your hike
and build some rock art, using glue and paint.

c) Rock Chalk
Some rocks will draw on pavement like chalk. Can you
find one?

• •

Book Resource Tips:
If You Are a Fossil Hunter, Byrd Baylor
Everybody Needs a Rock, Byrd Baylor
Rocks and Minerals, Eyewitness Books
Journey to the Center of the Earth, The Magic School Bus
series, Joanna Cole

✐ Travel Tip 70

Desert Life

• **all ages**
• **science and geography skills**

If you will be driving through or visiting a desert, acquaint
your children with the habitats and wildlife of its unusual
ecosystems. It's estimated that approximately 5 percent of
the earth's surface is desert. Many zoos have desert-life

exhibits. Build a desert garden using a terrarium or box planter. Layer sand, potting soil, rocks, and small stones. Plant a variety of cacti. To illustrate the heat of the desert, shine a lamp on the terrarium and let your child feel how it heats up. If you're an animal lover, add a lizard to the terrarium.

• •

Resource Tips:

If you're in the Tucson area, don't miss the Arizona-Sonora Desert Museum, the world-famous desert zoo and arboretum.

The Desert Is Theirs, Byrd Baylor (Atheneum), picture book to introduce young children to the desert.

One Day in the Desert, Jean Craighead George (HarperTrophy), a book for middle readers about an intensely hot experience in the desert.

Mojave, Diane Siebert (HarperCollins), picture book about the vast Mojave Desert.

Travel Tip 71
Leaving on a Jet Plane

Airport Games

- **all ages**
- **science and observational skills**

Airports are crossroads of language and culture. Many

airports offer tours to groups of children. Organize one for your neighborhood before your trip to acquaint your child with the flying process.

While you're waiting for your plane to depart, visit the observation tower. Encourage your child to take pictures for their "windows book" (Tip #59). Watch planes land and speculate where they've come from and where they may be going. Be a people watcher and observe clothing styles. Do you think that man in shorts just came from Florida? I'll bet that woman in the heavy coat has flown in from Minnesota. Are there people around you speaking a foreign language? Can you identify the language? Walk by the customs area and acquaint your child with the process of flying to another country. The airport is full of possibilities for an "I spy" game while you're waiting for your plane to depart. Point out machines to haul and load baggage, fuel trucks, food and beverage trucks, and all the attendants on the ground wearing earphones and directing planes.

When you board the airplane, ask to visit with the captain in the cockpit. Most are very hospitable to children and will let them spend a few minutes observing the cockpit. Some captains will even let your child announce the cruising altitude or weather patterns to the passengers over the PA system. Consult your flight attendant.

✎ Travel Tip 72

Planes, Trains, and Automobiles

- **all ages**
- **science and math skills**

How many modes of transportation can you take on your trip? Keep a log. Ask your child for suggestions: subways, taxis, ferryboats, sightseeing carriages, helicopters, airplanes, monorails, ships, steamrollers, trains, bikes, roller blades, buses, shuttles, trucks, horses, ski lifts, golf carts, wheelchairs, sleds. How are they different? Which holds the most people? The fewest people? Make a graph (see Tip #48) from slowest to fastest. Have him take out his stopwatch. How long does it take to go a mile in a buggy? How about a train? Which is the most fun? Which is highest? Lowest? Which is cheapest (perhaps your own two feet)? Which would he like to ride to school in every day? What would he like to own?

• •

Book Resource Tip:

This Is the Way We Go To School: A Book About Children Around the World, Edith Baer (Scholastic), shows school transportation for kids around the world.

You have a magic carpet
That will whiz you through the air;
to Spain or Maine or Africa
If you'll just tell it where.
So will you let it take you
Where you've never been before
Or will you buy some drapes to match
and use it
On the
Floor?

Shel Silverstein, *A Light in the Attic*

✐ Travel Tip 73

A Magnetic Experience

Magnet Play

- preschool, early school age
- science and language arts skills

supplies: metal board such as a cookie sheet or tray, small magnets with adhesive backs, construction paper.

As the miles roll by, help your children experiment with one of the basic forces of nature—magnetism. Explain some of the properties of magnets and many of their uses, such as the magnetic particles which cover your videocassette tape, allowing the image to appear on the screen. Remind them of their compass, of which a much larger version guides airplanes and ships safely to their destination. Magnets are at work all around us. There are many commercial magnet toys such as numbers and letters which will entertain children. A learning shop will have a good selection. Or make your own. Cut pieces of construction paper in a variety of shapes. You may want to laminate them to make them sturdier. Adhere a self-stick magnet to the back. Use a metal tray as a story board. Make magnetic tic-tac-toe characters, play hangman with magnetic letters. Kids can work addition and subtraction problems with magnetic numbers. Magnetic marbles can be purchased at learning stores, and they hold endless possibilities for sorting, counting, organizing by color, designing pictures, and playing games. One early childhood educator said that magnetic toys make a particularly good travel activity because the pieces are easily contained.

· ·

Resource Tip:
Magnadoodles make an excellent car toy.
MagnePoem, magnetic instant poetry kit, Illuminations
Tangoes, Rex Games, magnetic puzzle game
Smethport makes a variety of inexpensive magnetic toys and games.

Travel Tip 74

Collectibles

- **all ages**
- **science, organizational, and creative skills**

Kids love to collect, and traveling is a great time to begin or add to a collection. Seashells, state flags, pennants, pins, rocks, menus, ticket stubs, spoons, charms, snow globes, arrowheads, postcards, fossils, magnets, and coins are some of the many possibilities you will find along the way. Collections are important because they will later serve as reminders of your trip. Your youngster might want to spend some of his discretionary money on a collectible, or to reward himself for good behavior. Carry along some extra bags to fill with shells, rocks, or other interesting finds. Sorting and counting projects are a natural outgrowth of trip collections. How many different kinds of rocks did you collect? Categorize them into sizes. How about shells? When you return, your child will be very proud of his trip collection, and will want to add to it on future journeys. Use the collection as part of his museum display (Tip #83).

Books pertaining to your travel region, both fiction and nonfiction, can be great collectibles. Let your children choose a book about your destination that they can bring home. Every time they read the book it will bring back memories of the trip. Encourage them to take the book to school when they have a related unit of study.

* *

Resource Tip:
For more ideas about collecting and displaying, check *The Usborne Book of Collecting Things,* Kate Needam.

✎ Travel tip 75

Treasure Bag

- **all ages**
- **all skills depending on games and activities**

Delight your child with some trip surprises. Before departing, purchase or make several car games (see tip #26), books, and think up other travel activities. Cut several slips of paper and write treasure hints about each item or activity on a slip of paper. Put the surprises in one bag and the treasure hints in another bag. Have your child pick a treasure hint from the bag, read the hint, and guess what the treasure might be.

Treasure examples:
"Present this slip at the next gas stop,
and you may buy a _____(rhyming word)." (lollipop, soda pop)
"There are 52 of me and if you figure this one out you're a real joker." (new deck of cards—see Tip #49 for some games)
"I'm red, green, and purple all over and mark my words, I rub off." (new markers)
"Open me up and you will get
all the letters of the alphabet." (new book)
"These will come in handy at the beach
when the sun is bright.
So look me in the eye and think
until the answer comes to light." (new sunglasses.)

Depending on the length of your trip, you can offer a treasure every so many hours or miles. You won't need to remind them when time is up.

A friend recalled the time her mother gave her and her brother small whistles to take on a trip for entertainment. The whistles, however, were not entertainment for Driver Dad, who quickly snatched the whistles from their mouths and saved them for out-of-the-car blowing. You might want to bypass whistles for your treasure bag unless your nerves and eardrums are made of steel.

PART THREE

Travel Wise Making Memories

They're safely tucked in their own beds, but before the trip becomes a distant memory, take steps to savor your children's newly acquainted world. Whether you've returned from a cabin in the Adirondacks, the Waldorf in New York, a Florida beach condo, or a tent in the woods, you have memories to capture.

✎ Travel Tip 76

Picture This! Memory Book

- **all ages**
- **language arts and creativity skills**

Supplies: construction paper or scrapbook, staples or other fastener, pictures, brochures, and other memorabilia.

For a simple memory book for very young children, staple a few sheets of construction paper together and help them cut out and glue on trip pictures and other memorabilia. They can write, dictate, or illustrate captions for their book. Older children may want to organize a trip scrapbook from pictures they've taken and souvenirs they've collected along the way. You can laminate or cover the pages with clear contact paper. This scrapbook makes a great gift or addition to their childhood keepsake box.

✎ Travel Tip 77

Trip Alphabet Book

- **preschool, early school age**
- **language arts, memory, and creativity skills**

supplies: construction paper, bond paper, or index cards; glue, postcards; brochures, pictures, or any visuals from trip.

Staple together several sheets of paper and help your child choose visual reminders of the trip to make an alphabet book.

She can match pictures with letters as she remembers places you visited on your trip. Example: A = picture of the apple orchard, alligator from the zoo; f = farm or fish; s = statue, sand, and so on. She can label each picture with the alphabet word. She could also put her alphabet book on index cards. Punch holes in the corner of each card and fasten with a ring for an alphabet flip book. The alphabet trip book can be read over and over to reinforce early reading skills.

✎ Travel Tip 78

"All the News That's Fit To Print"

Family Travel Newspaper

- **school age**
- **language arts, geography, and history skills**

supplies: paper, scissors, typewriter, or computer

Encourage your children to make a newspaper of their trip either on the computer, or cut and pasted on sheets of paper and copied to send to family and friends. First, discuss with your children what goes into a newspaper. Show them a local newspaper and point out the different sections. What does she want to name her newspaper? "The Smith Family Travel Gazette"? "From Here to Wyoming"? "The Jones Travel Times"?

They can begin with a masthead of the publisher, editor, and reporters. Help each child pick a "beat," an area he wants to cover. Your baseball player would be a natural for writing the sports section about the professional baseball game he attended or the beach volleyball game he played in. The news and feature section could be written by each child as he chooses a highlight of the trip: seeing the Panda at Washington's National Zoological Park, reaching the summit of Pike's Peak, riding horses at a Montana ranch, viewing the original Plymouth Rock. The editorial section can feature issues such as beach or city pollution, traffic congestion, or safety, or if you're planning to mail copies to family and friends you visited, you could use this section for thank-you notes about their fine hospitality. Don't forget the entertainment section (perhaps movie and play reviews?) and of course, the comics.

Book Resource Tip:

Deadline! From News to Newspaper, Gail Gibbons (HarperCollins), gives a detailed description of what it takes to put a newspaper out on time.

A journey is best measured in friends rather than miles.
Tim Cahill, *Road Fever*

Travel Tip 79
Trip Collage

- **school age**
- **creativity and language arts skills**

supplies: poster or wooden board, paste, and varnish or lacquer

Collect pictures, posters, ticket stubs, menus, and any flat memorabilia from your trip. Have your children arrange their mementos along with notes from the trips—perhaps a page from their trip diary (Tip #32), the trip calendar (Tip #39), copy of the trip newspaper (Tip #48), or other trip comments. Glue them to a poster board or decoupage onto a piece of wood. To the wood, apply several layers of varnish or lacquer until the finish is smooth.

Travel Tip 80
"Where Did You Find Me?" Game

- **all ages**
- **memory and language arts skills**

supplies: paper sack and trip mementos

Gather several pictures and objects from your trip and put them in a paper bag. Play the "Where did you find me?" game. Have your child draw an object from the bag and see whether he can identify the object, remember where it came from, and talk about its significance. Example: "Oh, that was the shell we collected at Virginia Beach in front of our hotel just before we went to Busch Gardens. I remember we picked it up because it was the biggest one we saw." Or "That's a postcard of the Royal Gorge Suspension Bridge in Colorado. It's the tallest suspension bridge in the world. I remember when we went across the bridge we could see the bottom of the canyon through the cracks in the bridge. It was kinda spooky."

✎ Travel Tip 81

"Top 10 Reasons To Visit..."

Advertise Your Destination

- school age
- language arts, geography, history, and creativity skills

supplies: poster board, markers, and cutouts from magazines or travel brochures.

One of my favorite school projects (of the seemingly thousands) that my children have completed was a poster-board advertisement for a planet. The idea was to find out as much about your assigned planet as possible, and creatively entice your classmates to visit. My daughter came up with "Top Ten Reasons To Go to Neptune" which included, "It's an 'out of this world' experience," "Kite flying at its best (the wind blows over 600 miles an hour)," "No need for a refrigerator (it gets down to -350 degrees)" and "Great way to get away from your brother and sister—they'll never find you here!" It turned out to be a homework project that was more fun than "homework."

While not too many of us vacation on Neptune, the idea can be adapted for any destination. Your child can research your destination and use the information he's discovered to "advertise" its high points. Encourage him to be creative and use advertising slogans he's picked up from television and billboards.

Example:

"Baby it's cold up here"—Alaska.

"They're more than just faces in a crowd"—Mount Rushmore

"So, why would you want to visit Redwood National Park?" "Well, it's just a jungle out there. Two-hundred-foot-tall redwood and sequoia trees and all kinds of wildlife including the birds and elk."

Travel Tip 82
Shadowbox

- **all ages**
- **creativity and organizational skills**

The only thing more fun than collecting mementos throughout the trip is displaying them later. Save all your souvenirs, which may include ticket stubs, brochures, menus, shells, buttons, pins, matchbook covers (with the matches removed), postcards, and pennants, and mount them in a shadowbox. Shadowbox frames can be purchased at a hobby store, and your children can use their imaginations to create backdrops reflective of your trip. Once they mount the treasures to their satisfaction, they can label and date the items, or just let each one speak for itself. Regardless, it will be a conversation piece among their friends. Hang the shadow box in their room or family room.

Travel Tip 83
Make a Museum

- **school age**
- **geography, history, organizational, language arts, and science skills**

If your trip included museums, your children have learned about museum displays, the kinds of artifacts gathered for exhibits, and why people like to visit museums. They may want to create a trip museum of their own. This need not be complicated, and it will help them organize their trip souvenirs for an engaging display.

Activities:

a) Clear a desk or tabletop. Encourage them to arrange their trip items in groupings, keeping in mind some museum displays they have seen. All the postcards and posters displayed in one area, all the flags, pennants, and pins in another area. Trip pictures along with props that support the pictures such as shells for beach scenes should be arranged together. Any books on the travel region may also be exhibited. Baseball caps, T-shirts, or other wearable souvenirs can be arranged together. They can write labels and descriptions just as they saw in museums, along with a sign announcing "Smith Trip Museum." Invite friends, neighbors, and family members to visit your trip museum. For a really industrious museum curator, make a short brochure of items displayed and a short description of the item and how you came to purchase/collect it. Photograph the museum and send pictures to friends and family who helped make your trip a success along the way.

b) Rather than a tabletop, display your items in a large box for viewing from above. Make compartments as if you're looking down on museum rooms: the collectible room, which includes shells, pins, and fossils; the sports room, which holds pennants, ticket stubs, and a baseball; the family room, which holds pictures of family visited, an heirloom scarf obtained from Aunt Ann, a copy of the family tree from Tip #13.

Resource Tips:

🐾 *Doing Children's Museum: A Guide to 265 Hands-On Museums,* Joanne Cleaver (Williamson), is an indispensable guide to the many "learning playgrounds" that may be on your route.

🐾 *Make Your Own Museum: Guidebook/Galleries/Punch-Out Figures/Over 70 Works of Art,* Keith Godard, Andrea P.A. Belloli, is a hands-on museum kit which contains reusable stickers depicting works of art, galleries, and everything your child will need to create a model museum.

The board game *Masterpiece* (Parker Brothers) is a fast-paced introduction to the high-stakes world of fine art. For ages 8 and up.

Fun Travel Facts

Oddball Museums

The Barbie Hall of Fame features 16,000 dolls and other memorabilia, Palo Alto, Calif.

The Museum of Beverage Containers has over 40,000 beverage containers, Goodlettsville, Tenn.

The Nut Museum offers more than 100 species of nuts, Old Lyme, Conn.

Cypress Knee Museum displays a collection of artistic knotty growths on cypress-tree roots, Palmdale, Fla.

Lock Museum of America contains more than 23,000 locks, keys, and hardware, Terryville, Conn.

Marvin's Marvelous Mechanical Museum includes nickelodeon, pinball and slot machines, 400 video games, and rides, Farmington Hill, Mich.

Cookie Jar Museum features 2,000 cookie jars, Lemont, Ill.
Schmidt's Coca-Cola Museum offers 36,000 Coke items, Elizabethtown, Ky.
Yozeum is the ultimate yo-yo museum, Tucson, Ariz.

Source: Jerry Dunn, Family.com

✏ Travel Tip 84

Family "Been There" Map

- **all ages**
- **geography skills**

supplies: large world map, color star or dot stickers

Buy a large world map at your local book or map store. Frame it and hang the map on a wall in your home. Buy small star or dot stickers at a hobby shop. Place dots over places you have visited all over the world. Children will delight in showing off the map to their friends and naming far-flung destinations. Not only will they learn world geography, young map enthusiasts may chart your next

vacation. I have a friend who has such a map tastefully hung in her home's entryway. Few visitors step past the map without studying the dots and remarking on family travels around the world.

●●

Done with indoor complaints, querulous criticisms,
strong and content I travel the open road.
Walt Whitman, "Song of the Open Road"

✎ Travel Tip 85

Scenes from the Past

Diorama Making

- **all ages**
- **creativity skills**

supplies: shoe box, postcards, small craft accessories, items from your trip, cotton, glue, paint, crayons, or markers

Make a three-dimensional scene from your trip using a shoe box. Cut a hole at one end of the box. Remove the box lid and create a trip scene using postcards, or paint the background and glue on items obtained from your trip.

Activities:
Use shells and sand to make a beach scene. Glue on cotton for clouds and purchase small craft items such as cars and trees at a hobby shop to enhance a city scene. Buildings can

be drawn on the side of the box. Glue on small rocks and animals for a mountain scene or make a replica of a room you saw in a historical home, using furniture from a hobby shop. When the scene is finished, put the lid on and view the scene from the hole at the end of the box, or keep the lid off and view from above.

✎ Travel Tip 86

"Step in Time"

Vacation Stepping–stones

- all ages
- creativity and science skills

supplies: cement, individual pizza boxes, foil, trip collectibles

Make a keepsake stepping-stone for your garden. Purchase cement you can make at home from a building-supply store. Line an individual pizza box with foil. Pour in cement and decorate with shells, rocks, flower imprints, pin imprints, foreign currency, or handprints. After the cement is set, peel away the box and place the stone in your garden.

• •

PART FOUR

Travel Wise Anytime

✐ Travel Tip 87

Pen Friends

- **school age**
- **language arts and social skills**

Mail call is the high point of the day at my house. Encourage your child to become a pen pal with a distant friend or relative. Or locate a child who would like to be your child's pen pal through International Pen Friends, Dept. FS6, 1308 68th Lane North, Brooklyn, Minn. 55430; or Geomail, the National Geographic Pen Pal Network, a pen-pal club for English-speaking kids around the world. Write National Geographic Society, Dept. Geomail-OL, P. O. Box 96088, Washington, D.C. 20090-6088. School classes can also "adopt" another class and the children can exchange letters with other children far away about life in their school and city. Also, pen pals can be obtained on the Internet through Berits Best Sites for Children: Find a Pen Pal and from many of the Web sites listed in Tip #27. As always, be attentive to your child's Internet communication. Encourage your child to educate his pen pal about your region, and send photos and books that might interest him.

Of course, e-mail has revolutionized the concept of pen pals. If you have e-mail in your home, get addresses of family and friends around the country for instant communication. Grandparents, aunts and uncles are among the best pen pals for children. Encourage a lively exchange among several generations as a way to keep family stories alive. The best pen pal I ever had was my grandmother who sent me handmade Barbie clothes along with long letters. I camped at the mailbox waiting for her packages.

• •

I also wrote long letters to my pen pal in Phoenix, Arizona. Her name was Alice. My class had been exchanging letters with her class since school began. We were supposed to write once a month but I wrote at least once a week, ten, twelve, fifteen pages at a time. I represented myself to her as the owner of a palomino horse named Smiley who shared my encounters with mountain lions, rattlesnakes, and packs of coyotes on my father's ranch, the Lazy B. When I wasn't busy on the ranch I raised German shepherds and played for several athletic teams. Although Alice was a terse and irregular correspondent, I believed that she must be in awe of me, and imagined someday presenting myself at her door to claim her adoration.

Tobias Wolff, *This Boy's Life*

✎ Travel Tip 88

Postmark Collection

- **school age**
- **geography skills**

supplies: laminated map, small dot stickers

Perhaps North Pole, Alaska, is the most sought-after

postmark in the country, especially when Santa is making his list and checking it twice. New York City, Los Angeles, and Washington, D.C., may be the most common. Postmarks are something that we rarely notice, but they can provide some great geography lessons for children. As you travel, collect postmarks of the towns you visit. Encourage your children to check the mail for interesting postmarks. That junk mail shouldn't be thrown away until the postmark is checked and clipped. Have your children keep track of the many postmarks they collect by putting a small sticker dot on each town on a U. S. or world map. Perhaps they can get their friends or classmates to help collect and together they can plaster the world with dots. What postmark is the farthest away? What name is the most unusual? Can you collect postmarks from the town names in Tip #52? Graph the postmarks you receive over a one-month period of time.

✎ Travel Tip 89

Armchair Traveler

- **all ages**
- **language arts, history, geography, and creativity skills**

A hot summer day, the swimming pool closed, and you've heard, "Mom, I'm bored," one too many times. It's time to take a trip around the world. If you can't leave home, take the world to you. And you can go as far as your imagination will take you. Open an atlas, look at a globe or world map. Ask your children where they'd like to go. Select a state or country and begin mapping a route to take you there. Your children can make boarding passes, along with organizing an itinerary. Make a passport with a few sheets of paper stapled together, glue on a picture, and draw or put a stamp on countries you're "visiting."

What will you do on your imaginary trip? Do you have a budget (see Tip #17)? Visit the library and learn about local food and customs. What locations will you want to tour? What famous people are from the area/country? Learn about some games and crafts. Make a cave with chairs and sheets. Pack a backpack with a flashlight and food. Encourage youngsters to dress up as a "señorita" or "airplane pilot." Culminate the "trip" with a dinner (see Tip #10) that your child helps prepare.

Variation: So your kids can't wait to go to the beach? Have a beach day at home. Make some sand and shell rubbings. Bury some treasures in the sand box for them to find. Or put the hose in the sandbox to make sand castles and moats. Demonstrate floating and sinking with a tub of water. Do rocks float? Why not? Does your toy boat float? Why? What about a cork? Have him gather objects to see whether they sink or swim. Put a balloon on top of your sprinkler. Does the spray of water keep it in the air? How many can you keep in the air at once? Fill water balloons. Make a shell collage, necklace, or decorate a shell picture frame. Put some blue food coloring in clear soda and serve up some nice cool seawater along with some fish crackers. Or make some blue gelatin and before it completely sets, add some gummy fish. You'll have the whole neighborhood wanting to come on your "beach vacation."

Congratulations!
Today is your day.
You're off to a great place!
You're off and away.
You have brains in your head.
You have feet on your shoes.
You can steer yourself
Any direction you choose.
You're on your own. And you know what you know.
And YOU are the guy who'll decide where to go.

Dr. Suess, Oh, the Places You'll Go

✐ Travel Tip 90

Pretend Corner

- **preschool, early school age**
- **creativity and language arts skills**

Stock a pretend corner in your child's play area. In addition to the tutus and police hats, add some transportation and travel props, especially if you're going on a trip. A beach hat and sunglasses, a lei and grass skirt, an old fishing pole and waders, a sombrero, an airline captain's hat, any sports team mementos. The possibilities are endless. While you're adding props to the pretend corner, don't forget a big box. A refrigerator box to make a boxcar (see Tip #21) or airport is ideal. Boxes have a million uses for kids. They can make their own luggage or set up a museum to display their mementos. They can use several to make a skyscraper or hotel, or to make a time machine (see Tip #91).

Resource Tip:

Thrift shops or resale stores are great places to pick up costumes of all sorts.

✎ Travel Tip 91

A Wrinkle in Time

Time Machine Travel

- **all ages**
- **temporal, history, and language arts skills**

supplies: box (optional), gadgets from a hobby shop

Encourage your young child to make a time machine out of a large box. For decorations, visit a hobby shop and let her pick out some gadgets such as knobs, pie cleaners, or sparkle paint, or clean out some of your junk drawers and donate spools, lids, cans, and buttons. Older children might want to forgo the box project and just play the game. If you were going back in time, whom would you like to meet? Name 10 people from different eras. Plot them on your time line (Tip #16). If George Washington lived in your house, what would most surprise him? What would be fun about living in his era? Perhaps riding horseback. Take a walk around your neighborhood and speculate what it might have looked like 100 years ago. What might it look like in 100 years? Children will have a difficult time understanding the length of 100 years, so put it in context. The time line will help. Their grandparents may be around 75 years old. Their state may be around 100 years old. Talk about events that happened around 100 years ago.

Variation: Talk to your child about important historical events such as slavery and the Civil War, plot them on your time line, and ask your child, "If you could travel in your time machine back to those events, how would you change them?" This offers important value lessons as well as history lessons.

• •

Book Resource Tip:
    The children's classic, *A Wrinkle in Time,* Madeleine L'Engle (Yearling), is a great school-age book to go with this exercise.

✎ Travel Tip 92

Travel Bee

• **school age**
• **geography, history, and language arts skills**

You've participated in spelling bees. How about a family travel bee? Test your own family's travel recall with rounds organized like an old-fashioned spelling bee. The bee might include age-appropriate questions in the following format:

Geography Round—questions about states, mountain ranges, national parks you've visited. What states make up the four corners? What is the northernmost state of the lower forty-eight? What mountain range did we ski on in Colorado?

History Round—questions about historical figures, homes, monuments, and events you've learned about on your trips. What was the name of the Civil War Battlefield we visited? What state was partly settled in land runs? What is the name of Thomas Jefferson's home?

Trivia Round—questions about unusual facts you learned along the way. Who was the first president to sleep in the White House? What was the name of the largest fish we saw at the aquarium?

Family Fun Round—questions pertaining to humorous (or otherwise) family incidents on your trip. What city did Mom get lost in? What was the name of the lake we fished in? How many different swimming pools did we swim in on our trip?

✎ Travel Tip 93

Planting a Seed

- all ages
- science skills

While on your trip, notice the native vegetation. Buy or gather some wildflower or vegetable seeds for a backyard garden. Explore natural settings on your trip, and as you wander look for plants that have gone to seed. Collect the seeds and store them in separate, labeled containers. When you return home, the seeds can be dried and planted or frozen for next season. Sometimes museum or gift shops sell seed packets of native vegetation. Seed and garden catalogs and gardening magazines are useful to show what will grow well in your area. Select a small garden spot with the appropriate amount of sunshine and good soil, and plant your trip garden. As your garden blooms, you can watch the many critters it will attract. Add a garden stepping-stone (Tip #86), a birdbath, or bird feeder for your own wildlife garden spot.

Or, if an outside garden is too daunting, let your child have a window-box garden in her room using a half-gallon paper milk carton, cut in half and filled with potting soil.

• •

As parents, we can take our children with us to the land. We can be there with them as they climb on rocks, play in streams and waves, dig in the rich soil of woods and gardens, putter and learn. Here, on the land, we learn from each other. Here, our children's journey begins.

Stephen Trimble, *The Geography of Childhood,*
Gary Paul Nabhan and Stephen Trimble

✎ Travel Tip 94

Travel Publisher

- **school age**
- **language arts skills**

Many children's magazines love to hear from their readers. Encourage your child to send in one of her trip poems or stories for possible publication. Check several magazines that might be appropriate, or write to the magazine to get a copy of writers' guidelines. Encourage her to write a letter to be published in the "Letters from Readers" section of her favorite magazine about a unique travel spot and recommend it to other kids. Many local newspapers have a kids' section. Check with the editor to see whether your child might submit something about her travel experience. In the third grade, my brother wrote a poem about a penguin and it was published in *Highlights Magazine*. He can still recite the poem on the spot for anyone interested. It's always fun to see your name in print, and you never know what literary giants may grow from that first publication.

Where you might publish your travel stories:

Children's Express, 20 Charles St., N.Y., 10014, a news service reported by kids 13 and under.

Children's Magic Window, 6125 Olson Memorial, Minn., 55422. Kid stuff pages that publish letters, poems, and stories.

Creative Kids, GCT, Mobile, Ala., 36660 publishes children's works.

Jack and Jill, P.O. Box 567, Indianapolis, Ind., publishes children's stories, poems, and jokes for grades two through six.

Stone Soup, The Magazine for Children, P. O. Box 83, Santa Crux, Calif. 95063, is a bimonthly magazine of writing

...... by children.

Children's Digest, 1100 Waterway Blvd. P.O. Box 567, Indianapolis, Ind., publishes stories, poems, and jokes from children.

The Children's Magazine, 8655 East Via DeVentura, Suite G-150, Scottsdale, Ariz., 85258, showcases the writing talents of children by publishing their stories and poems.

Cricket, 315 Fifth Street, Peru, Ill. 61354 prints children's letters and sponsors children's writing contests.

✎ Travel Tip 95

Travel Magazines

- **all ages**
- **language arts, geography, and history skills**

Subscribe to some travel and nature magazines that both you and your children might enjoy. There are many good magazines for adults such as *National Geographic's Traveler; Travel & Leisure; Southern Living; Conde Nast Traveler; Roads to Adventure, The Magazine of Family Camping; Sierra: Exploring, Enjoying and Protecting the Planet; Outpost: The Traveller's Journal.* For children: *Wild Outdoor World, Your Big Backyard, Ranger Rick, Cobblestone—The History Magazine for Young People,* among many good ones. Let your children cut pictures from the magazines for posters, scrapbooks, and reference material. Consider enrolling your children as junior members of the National Geographic Society. They will receive a copy of *National Geographic World,* a magazine written for children ages 8-14, posters, trading cards, and activity booklets. The cost is $17.95. The phone number is 1-800-437-5521.

✐ Travel Tip 96

Travel Software

- **all ages**
- **all academic skills**

   Browse through computer and parenting magazines and software stores, and check with your child's computer teacher about good choices in the latest children's software related to history, geography, and travel. There are many choices, and new ones are developed constantly. Some recommended software:

Where in the USA Is Carmen Sandiego? Broderbund Software, ages 10 and up

Where in the World Is Carmen Sandiego? Broderbund Software, ages 10 and up

Where in America's Past Is Carmen Sandiego? Broderbund Software, ages 10 and up

Map Skills, Optimum Resource, ages 7-9

American Adventure, Knowledge Adventure, ages 8 and up

Oregon Trail games, MECC, ages 8 and up

Swamp Gas Visits the United States of America, Inline software, ages 8 and up

Eco-Adventures in the Oceans, Chariot Software, ages 10 and up

The United States is Missing, Instructional Fair, ages 9 and up

GeoSafari makes geography, history, and science software for children

Time Machine Travel, Instructional Fair, ages 9 and up

Wild Western Town, Fisher Price, ages 3-7

✎ Travel Tip 97

Congressional Pages

- **high school students**
- **government and history skills**

When I was in high school, I spent a week in the Oklahoma legislature as a page. I had a beginning interest in government and politics, so my parents contacted our state senator and arranged for me to spend a week at the state capital along with many other high school students from around the state. I can't brag that I went on to any great political career or became involved in any government work, but politics has always held a fascination for me. Just fetching water for the powerful movers and shakers is quite an experience for a high school student.

A friend of mine from the southwest planned an annual trip to Washington, D.C., while her children were growing up. When her daughter was in high school, she applied and was accepted as a page in the U.S. Congress. Her mother said her early travels to Washington, D.C., inspired her political interest. You never know what travel experience might spark a future career. Every year, students from all over the country are selected as pages in their legislatures as well as U. S. Congress. Contact your state or U. S. senator or representative about the application process for such positions.

Travel Tip 98

Foreign Visitors

Even if you can't travel internationally, you can bring an international flavor to your family. Host a foreign exchange student. Perhaps your church sponsors missionaries. When they visit, invite them to stay with you, especially if they have children. Ask them to share stories about their life in the mission field. Or perhaps your church hosts visiting choirs. Offer to put up some of the students in your home. Bring out-of-town business associates to meet your children. Use the opportunity to talk about where your guest is from and exchange cultural differences. Invite guests to Thanksgiving, Hanukkah, or other family celebrations and ask them to share holiday experiences from their culture and country. You don't have to travel to Israel to learn a great deal about your heritage, ancestors, and religion. Your home can be a crossroads of many cultural exchanges.

• •

Resource Tip:

For information about hosting a foreign student or living abroad, check www.afs.org, the American Field Service Web site.

✏ Travel Tip 99

Travel Box

- **school age**
- **history and organizational skills**

supplies: appropriate size keepsake box and trip mementos, acid-free paper

When you travel, keep your eye out for mementos that might be helpful during a unit of study at school. When we were in Philadelphia visiting Independence Hall, we stopped in the gift shop and bought a reproduction of the Declaration of Independence and Bill of Rights. I figured they would come in handy when my children studied American history. After your trip, help your child corral all his mementos in a keepsake box. You might want to purchase an archival safe box to store the mementos (it can be purchased from Light Impressions catalog, 1-800-828-6216). Newspapers, pictures, brochures, programs, and postcards can be stored and easily retrieved when your child wants to refer to his box for a school project. The keepsake box can become a "time capsule" where you store your precious trip mementos. As your children grow and the box or boxes fill, pull them out from time to time and relive their childhood adventures with them.

✏ Travel Tip 100

Local Travel

- **all ages**
- **all academic skills**

Take a trip down the road. A family vacation doesn't have to be out of state or even out of town. How many times have we all said, "The only time we visit the local tourist attractions is when we have company." Choose five local attractions you've never visited and plan a trip. Seek out local tours, museums, orchards, historical homes, nature preserves, buildings, monuments, parks, pumpkin patches, and festivals. Pretend you're a tourist in your own town. We become so familiar with our surroundings that we forget about the wealth of travel potential in our own backyards. I live 25 miles from the Will Rogers Memorial. Have I ever taken my children to visit? No, I am embarrassed to say. They've been to the Lincoln Memorial and the Wright Brothers Memorial, but not to the one down the road. I'll have to remedy that shortly.

Check with your local chamber of commerce, bookstore, telephone book, or library for information about unusual local destinations. Perhaps you've visited all the hands-on museums and other obvious attractions, but there are probably many more with which you may be unfamiliar. Is there a garden center in your area? What about homes registered on the National Register of Historic Places? Can you pick your own strawberries, peaches, or blueberries at a local farm? Does your local theater give "behind the scenes" tours? Organize a group to visit the kitchen of a local pizza parlor. During the summer, play "tourist" one day a week and choose an interesting site to visit—maybe a new park on the other side of town—that may be off your beaten path. Encourage your children to scout around for local adventures and help plan the outing.

PART FIVE

• •

Travel Wise Resources

✎ Travel Tip 101
Recommended Books and Resources

The following list recommends books from all regions of the United States. It is by no means comprehensive, as there are hundreds of regional books from which to choose. The following represent many appropriate selections, both fiction and nonfiction, to offer your children a glimpse of the travel experience that awaits them.

Northeast
early school age/picture books
Blueberries for Sal, Robert McCloskey (Viking)
Jenny's Journey, Sheila White Samton (Puffin)
Make Way for Ducklings, Robert McCloskey (Viking)
One Morning in Maine, Robert McCloskey (Viking)
The Puffins Are Back, Gail Gibbons (HarperCollins)
Riptide, Frances Ward Weller (Philomel)
The Star-Spangled Banner, Peter Spier (Yearling)

school-age books
Abigail's Drum, John A. Minahan (Pippin)
A Baker's Dozen: A Colonial American Tale, Heather Forest (Voyager)
By the Dawn's Early Light: The Story of the Star-Spangled

Banner, Stephen Kroll (Scholastic)

The Courage of Sarah Noble, Alice Dalgliesh (Atheneum)

The Cricket in Times Square, George Selden (Farrar Straus Giroux)

Finest Kind O'Day: Lobstering in Maine, Bruce McMillan (Apple Island)

The Fledgling, Jane Langton (HarperCollins)

The Fragile Flag, Jane Langton (HarperCollins)

From the Mixed-Up Files of Mrs. Basil E. Frankweiler, E.L. Konigsburg (Atheneum)

From Path to Highway: The Story of the Boston Post Road, Gail Gibbons (HarperCollins)

Hannah's Fancy Notions: A Story of Industrial New England, Pat Ross (Puffin)

The Inside-Outside Book of New York City, and *The Inside-Outside Book of Washington D.C.*, Roxie Munro (Putnam)

Johnny Tremain, Esther Forbes (Houghton Mifflin)

Legend of Sleepy Hollow, Washington Irving (Troll)

Lily and Miss Liberty, Carla Stevens (Little Apple)

Little Women, Louisa May Alcott

Lost on a Mountain in Maine, Donn Fendler (Beach Tree Books)

My Side of the Mountain, Jean Craighead George (Dutton)

Paul Revere's Ride, Henry Wadsworth Longfellow (Puffin)

And Then What Happened, Paul Revere?, Jean Fritz (Coward McCann)

Tituba of Salem Village, Ann Petry (HarperCollins)

Sarah Bishop, Scott O'Dell (Houghton Mifflin)

The Sign of the Beaver, Elizabeth George Speare (Houghton Mifflin)

Soup, Robert Newton Peck (Yearling)

Sybil Rides for Independence, Drollene P. Brown (Albert Whitman)

What's the Big Idea Ben Franklin? Jean Fritz (Putnam)
The Witch of Blackbird Pond, Elizabeth George Speare (Houghton Mifflin)

Mid-Atlantic
early school-age picture book
The Sea Is Calling Me, poems selected by Lee Bennett Hopkins (Harcourt Brace)
The Story of the White House, Kate Waters (Scholastic)

school-age books
The Blue Hill Meadows, Cynthia Rylant (Harcourt Brace)
The Buck Stops Here: The Presidents of the United States, Alice Provensen (Harcourt Brace)
Clara and the Bookwagon, Nancy Smiler Levinson (HarperTrophy)
Ida Early Comes Over the Mountain, Robert Burch (Puffin)
The Island of Wild Horses, Jack Denton Scott and Ozzie Sweet (Putnam)
Misty of Chincoteague, Marguerite Henry (Aladdin)
No Star Nights, Anna Egan Smucker (Knopf)
Paddle-to-the-Sea, Holling C. Holling (Houghton Mifflin)
Shiloh, Phyllis Naylor (Yearling)
A Visit to Washington D.C., Jill Krementz (Scholastic)
When I Was Young in the Mountains, Cynthia Rylant (Dutton)

Midwest
early school-age picture books
Heartland, Diane Siebert (Crowell)

school-age books
Addie Across the Prairie, Laurie Lawlor (Minstrel)
Caddie Woodlawn, Carol Ryrie Brink (Aladdin)
Humbug Mountain, Sid Fleischman (Yearling)
Little House on the Prairie (one of several in a series), Laura

Ingalls Wilder
Paul Bunyan/ Pecos Bill /Johnny Appleseed, Steven Kellogg (Morrow)
Tom Sawyer and *Huckleberry Finn,* Mark Twain
Wagon Wheels, Barbara Brenner (HarperCollins)
Weasel, Cynthia Defelice (Atheneum)
Wild Weather: Tornadoes! Lorraine Jean Hopping (Cartwheel Books)
Wizard of Oz, Frank Baum

Southeast
Strawberry Girl, Lois Lenski (HarperCollins)
The Wright Brothers at Kitty Hawk, Donald Sobol

South
early school-age picture books
The Story of Ruby Bridges, Robert Coles (Scholastic)

school-age books
To Be a Slave, Julius Lester (Scholastic)
From the Hills of Georgia: An Autobiography in Paintings, Mattie Lou O'Kelly (Little Brown)
Letters from a Slave Girl: The Story of Harriet Jacobs, Mary E. Lyons (Aladdin)
Roll of Thunder, Hear My Cry, Mildred D. Taylor (Puffin)
Sounder, William H. Armstrong, (HarperCollins)
Walking the Road to Freedom, Jeri Ferris (Carolrhoda)
Which Way Freedom?, Joyce Hansen (Camelot)

Southwest
early school-age picture book
Cowboys, Lucille Recht Penner (Grosset and Dunlap)
Frida Maria: A Story of the Old Southwest, Deborah Nourse Lattimore (Voyager)

The Legend of the Bluebonnet, Tomie DePaola (Putnam)
Roxaboxen, Alice McLerran (Lothrop)

school-age books
Angels in the Dust, Margot Theis Raven (Bridgewater)
Hawk, I'm Your Brother, Byrd Baylor (Atheneum)
Old Yeller, Fred Gipson (HarperCollins)
Rattlesnake Run, Keo Felker Lazarus (Follett)
Tree in the Trail, Holling C. Holling (Houghton)
Where the Red Fern Grows, Wilson Rawls (Doubleday)
The White Stallion, Elizabeth Shub (Bantam)

West
early school-age picture books
Dakota Dugout, Ann Turner (Aladdin)
Charlie Drives the Stage, Eric A. Kimmel (Holiday)
The Josefina Story Quilt, Eleanor Coerr (HarperCollins)
Mojave, Diane Siebert (HarperCollins)
Wagons West!, Roy Gerrard (Farrar Straus Giroux)
Rosie and the Rustlers, Roy Gerrard (Farrar Straus Giroux)
Westering, Alice Putnam (Lodestar Books)
The Zebra-Riding Cowboy: A Folk Song from the Old West,
collected by Angela Shelf Medearis (Owlet)

school-age books
Between Two Worlds, Candice Ransom (Apple)
The Black Pearl, Scott O'Dell (Houghton Mifflin)
Brighty of the Grand Canyon, Marguerite Henry (Aladdin)
Cowboys of the Wild West and *Children of the Wild West*,
Russell Freedman (Clarion)
Dragonwings, Laurence Yep (HarperCollins)
Frontier Home, Raymond Bial (Houghton Mifflin)
The Girl Who Loved Wild Horses, Paul Goble (Aladdin)
The Incredible Journey of Lewis and Clark, Rhoda Blumberg

(Beech Tree Books)
A Jar of Dreams, Yoshiko Uchida (Aladdin)
Stone Fox, John Reynolds Gardiner (Crowell)
Waterless Mountain, Laura Armer (Knopf)

Northwest
early school-age picture books
The Boy Who Lived With the Seals, retold by Rafe Martin (Putnam)
A Caribou Alphabet, Mary Beth Owens (Sunburst)
Lucky Hares and Itchy Bears, Susan Ewing (Alaska Northwest Books)
Nessa's Fish and *Nessa's Story*, Nancy Luenn (Atheneum)

school-age books
Anna's Athabaskan Summer, Arnold Griese (Boyds Mills Press)
Black Star, Bright Dawn, Scott O'Dell (Houghton Mifflin)
Gentle Ben, Walt Morey (Puffin)
Go Home River, James Magdanz (Alaska Northwest Books)
Julie of the Wolves, Jean Craighead George (HarperCollins)
Tiktala, Margaret Shaw-MacKinnon (Holiday)
Volcano: The Eruption and Healing of Mount St. Helens, Patricia Lauber (Simon & Schuster)

Book Series
America the Beautiful series (Children's Press, Chicago)
Childhood of Famous Americans series (Aladdin), biography series
The Landmark History of the American People, Daniel J. Boorstin (Random House)
The History of Us, Joy Hakim (Oxford)
Terrific Topics (Carson-Dellosa Publishing Company, Inc.), which includes subjects such as transportation, ocean, farm, and woodland animals)
Creative Teaching Press, Inc., has a theme series including

topics such as transportation, deserts, grandparents, North American Indians

The Magic School Bus series, Joanna Cole (Scholastic)

General Resources

AAA TourBooks provide a wealth of information about the history, geography, recreation, and points of interest as well as all manner of travel-planning help. Contact your local AAA for more information.

Zoos, Anthony D. Marshall (Random House), lists 102 zoos, aquariums, and wildlife parks across the United States.

The Early America Sourcebook: A Travelers Guide, Chuck Lawliss (Crown), for a guide to historical destinations.

America's Historic Places, Michael Lewis for National Geographic Society Book Division, a guide to more than 2,500 of the best historic sites in fifty states with introductions to people, places and events

Wish You Were Here: Emily's Guide to the 50 States, Kathleen Krull (Bantam), kid-friendly guide to traveling across the United States.

Geography from A to Z: A Picture Glossary, Jack Knowlton, an introduction to geography for young children

It Happened in America: True Stories from the Fifty States, Lila Perl (Henry Holt), offers trivia and a short history of each state along with attractive destinations.

Free Stuff for Kids, Meadowbrook Press, is a great resource for obtaining stickers, flags, decals, maps, etc. The world is full of freebies for kids. Take advantage of them. Many tourism bureaus, chambers of commerce, airlines, factories, and travel agencies have free mementos they love to pass on to kids.